Schools under Scrutiny

Schools under Scrutiny

The Case of Northern Ireland

Edited by Leslie Caul

MACMILLAN
EDUCATION

First published 1990

Published by
MACMILLAN EDUCATION LTD
Houndmills, Basingstoke, Hampshire RG21 2XS
and London
Companies and representatives
throughout the world

Printed in Hong Kong

British Library Cataloguing in Publication Data
Schools under scrutiny: the case of Northern Ireland.
1. Northern Ireland. Schools
I. Caul, Leslie
371.009416
ISBN 0-333-51115-8

Contents

PART I   Educational Development or at least leave it as it is

PART II   Practise What You Preach

PART III   Issues Facing Schools in Northern Ireland

Tables

Figures

Figures

List of Contributors

H. Rex Cathcart is a Professor of Education at the Queen's University, Belfast

Anne Sutherland is a Research Fellow at the Northern Ireland Council for Educational Research, Belfast

Alex McEwan is a Senior Lecturer at the School of Education, Queen's University, Belfast

Leslie Caul is a Lecturer at Stranmillis College, Belfast

Joan Harbison is a Lecturer at Stranmillis College, Belfast

Jean Whyte is a Lecturer at Trinity College, Dublin

Sean Vallely is Acting Director at the Northern Ireland Council for Educational Development, Belfast

Anne O'Shea is the Director of the 11–16 Programme, Belfast

Peter Daws is Dean of Education at the University of Ulster, Coleraine

Dermot McCartan is a Development Officer with the Regional Curriculum Base, Jordanstown

Jim Billingsley is Principal of King's Park Primary School, Newtownabbey

Peter McGaffin was Principal of Hazelwood Integrated Primary School, Belfast

Gerry Ruddy is a teacher at Corpus Christi College, West Belfast

Emma Caul is Principal of Bruslee Primary School, Newtownabbey

Abbreviations

ACE	Advisory Committee for Education
ACT	All Children Together
AGBVGS	Association of Governing Bodies of Voluntary Grammar Schools
APU	Assessment of Performance Unit
BE	Basic Education
BELB	Belfast Education and Library Board
BELTIE	Belfast Charitable Trust for Integrated Education
CDT	Craft, Design and Technology
CPVE	Community Programme of Vocational Education
CSE	Certificate of Secondary Education
CTC	City Technology College
DED	Department of Economic Development
DENI	Department of Education for Northern Ireland
DES	Department of Education and Science
EC	European Community
ELB	Education and Library Board
EMU	Education for Mutual Understanding
ESN	Educationally Sub-Normal
FE	Further Education
GTC	Government Training Centres
ILEA	Inner London Education Authority
LA	Courses for the Less Able
NEELB	North Eastern Education and Library Board
NICED	Northern Ireland Council for Educational Development
NICER	Northern Ireland Council for Educational Research
PPC	Primary Programme Committee
PPRU	Public Policy Research Unit
RCB	Regional Curriculum Base
SED	Scottish Education Department
TRAWL	Transition to Adult and Working Life

VEP	Vocational Educational Programme
WPC	Work Preparation Centres
YTP	Youth Training Programme
YW	Youthways

EDITOR'S PREFACE

'Schools under Scrutiny' is divided into three parts. Part I sets the contemporary scene analysing curriculum development in Northern Ireland. This section analyses how primary and secondary education was apparently restructured in the 1980s. Part II looks at the practice of schools in the province. In particular this section analyses school management and focuses sharply on innovation, opening a ..ew integrated school and teaching disaffected youth. Part III provides an analysis of the four major issues in education in the province. These themes include selection for secondary education, religious segregation, teaching in a small school and disaffected youth.

Part I considers an overview of education in Northern Ireland. In a critical and illuminating analysis Rex Cathcart discusses the political structures of education. Cathcart shows how British inspired educational reform was reinterpreted by vested interests in the province and used as a means of maintaining an existing set of power relations.

One aspect of the work of the Northern Ireland Council for Educational Development is analysed by its Acting Director, Sean Vallely. Vallely describes how NICED developed a strategic approach to the production of a set of curriculum guidelines for primary schools. The Primary Guidelines arose from a request from the main teaching unions for a clear definition of educational goals. It was not surprising that the embedded traditionalism of educational practice led to a set of subject based booklets. What was remarkable was the process prescribed for implementation. The strongly traditional subject based guidelines were to be 'implanted' in individual schools through a process of top-down review. Each primary school was asked initially to review its practice through the construction of a statement of aims. The subject guidelines were then to be set into this framework. It was argued that a school could consider one or two subject guidelines per annum. NICED enlisted the support of the province's management authorities who as Vallely describes played an active role in implementation.

In the secondary school sector continuing pupil disaffection and low attainment in the non-grammar school sector led to a number of initiatives. Two curriculum based approaches to the work of the secondary school, including grammar schools, became prominent in the 1980s. The 11–16 Programme set in motion a systematic review of secondary school practice. TRAWL, on the other hand, reviewed the more instrumental aspects of schooling and is described by Peter Daws in Chapter 4.

In Chapter 3 Anne O'Shea sets the structure of the 11–16 Programme into a description of secondary education in Northern Ireland. Sister Anne, a former grammar school principal, argues most forcibly that schools are failing to provide for the needs of young people today. She identifies the organisation of schools, their academic leaning and their inbuilt resistance to change as factors limiting their contribution in the 1980s. Again tied to a 'whole school review' model the 11–16 Programme, of which O'Shea was the director, attemped to improve the quality of delivery of individual schools. O'Shea sets out the philosophy of the programme and describes how the process was to incorporate all secondary schools in the province through a rolling programme. The chapter ends with an interesting analysis of the progress made to date and with a comment on a common curriculum.

In Part II Jim Billingsley discusses the implementation of NICED Primary Guidelines. Billingsley, a primary school principal, questions the model used by the Guidelines for innovation. He feels that the initiative lacked the flexibility that would have enabled schools to use an alternative approach, namely a 'practice into aims' model. This alternative, Billingsley argues, would have avoided many of the pitfalls that NICED encountered. In Chapter 8 Emma Caul suggests that it is one thing to examine school policy and to begin to consider each subject systemically, it is another issue to oversee innovation in classroom practice. Possibly Billingsley begins from this point of view in arguing for the creation of a school climate that would encourage ongoing reflection of teaching by classroom practitioners.

The thorny question of integrated education is discussed by Peter McGaffin. In an interesting and extremely honest account McGaffin describes how he managed and directed the opening of an Integrated Primary School in Greater Belfast. McGaffin shows how important religious education is in Northern Ireland and how altruism, no matter how well intended, can often fail to recognise the harsh pragmatism involved in managing a school.

If Integrated Education has a middle-class bias, Gerry Ruddy highlights another aspect of schooling in the province. In a series of short notes written for colleagues Ruddy provides an insight into working with less able children in west Belfast. This is a special case where urban decay and industrial poverty have become embroiled with terrorism and street violence. Ruddy illustrates an approach which encourages empathy with the adolescents. His approach relates low self-esteem, disruptive behaviour and poor academic achievement.

The work of a teaching principal is described by Emma Caul who places the role of the principal of the small school in context. Emma Caul combines a diary describing her teaching in a rural primary school with an account of managing the school. She places ongoing school rationalisation and closure high on the neighbourhood's agenda and illustrates how closure is inevitable for the majority of small rural primary schools.

The development of 'Youthways', an early example of working with 'at risk' young people, is analysed by Dermot McCartan. He places his account into a framework of increasing youth unemployment and growing normlessness. 'Youthways' was piloted as a programme of education, work experience and training and became a formative part of Youth Training. The programme was organised around four themes: Skills and Practices, Communication Studies, Industrial and Environmental Studies and General Activities. While providing a model for YTP itself, 'Youthways' was forced to adapt to change as it became a part of the wider training scenario. McCartan emphasises the importance of tutor/student relationships, project work and counselling as integral aspects of the course. The courses were of particular concern as they were targeted at young people who had come into contact with paramilitary organisations and street violence. It is a part of life in Northern Ireland not to think it strange that several Belfast and Derry colleges institutionalise sectarianism by having separate YTP courses for Catholics and Protestants. While the socio-cultural identity of the young people may be different the problems are similar.

Accounts of practice suggest that there are four major issues facing education in Northern Ireland. Firstly, this is the only part of the United Kingdom to have retained selection at eleven and separate grammar schools since 1947. The 1947 Education Act (NI) was the equivalent of the Butler Act (1944) in England and Wales. Secondly, because of the large Catholic minority in the province, a tradition has grown up whereby education is segregated strictly by religion. With the heightening of feelings in the 1970s about a divided society attempts are now being made to lessen cultural differences. In education this movement has addressed the question of integrated schools. Thirdly, the transfer of Protestant primary schools, especially, although not exclusively so, located in rural areas has left the state a legacy of small schools. Nevertheless continual rationalisation in the primary school sector has been unable to reduce significantly the number of schools with a 'teaching principal'. Finally, although the numbers are declining a large proportion of young people still leave secondary school without any certificated qualifications whatsoever. Selective, segregated and small schools with a high proportion of under-achieving young people typifies an educational system in a divided society.

In Chapter 10 Anne Sutherland considers the selective system when she outlines the history of segregation of pupils at eleven by ability. Sutherland looks at the effects of selection on the primary school curriculum and on the perceived importance of English and mathematics. The time schools spend on coaching for the tests is evaluated and set against the popularly held view of an 11+ dominated curriculum. Sutherland argues cogently that the Transfer Procedure is commonly used as a popular scapegoat for a lack of a creative and imaginative approach to the curriculum in primary schools. At the secondary level the selective system has polarised the bipartite curriculum. For borderline pupils opportunities can be lost through an absence of modern language and sciences in the non-grammar school sector.

In an exploratory analysis of how schooling transmits deeply structural aspects of identity, Alex McEwen (Chapter 11) examines the dissimilarities existing between the two cultural traditions in the province. McEwen illustrates how the struggle for identity has become a major facet of schooling and is reflected in the curriculum, para-curriculum and management of the different school types. In placing integrated education into the context of a selective and religiously segregated system, McEwen poses the question; will this involvement lead to the emergence of a new identity where Catholics and Protestants can be seen to be as of equal worth?

In an analysis of small primary schools Leslie Caul (Chapter 12) compares curricular provision in Northern Ireland with a number of small schools in Scotland. The debate about the future of the small school is set into a framework which suggests that such schools are no longer viable for curricular, social, economic and professional reasons. Caul argues that in terms of curriculum there is little that distinguishes the small school from the larger school. Teachers appear to be equally concerned about the importance of academic achievement in English and mathematics and of the need to foster a happy and secure learning environment. Schools in Northern Ireland are shown to be subject dominated and to be more concerned about intellectual development than their Scottish counterparts.

The case of under-achievement is reviewed by Joan Harbison in Chapter 13 where she describes persistent non-attendance in the Belfast conurbation. From 1977 'condoned absenteeism' has been an important aspect of non-attendance at school. Harbison draws on a study of 'Condoned Absenteeism' carried out by Caul and Harbison (1986) in Belfast where the researchers compared parental and pupil perceptions of schooling. In this study Caul and Harbison show how early explanations of absenteeism failed to take account of the frame of reference of the pupil. In developing this theme Harbison argues that schools are not generally sensitive to, nor supportive of, the needs of adolescents. By becoming more aware of the perception of under-achievers schools can adjust their approach to young people who find themselves alienated from the formal scholastic hierarchy. This position Harbison believes can lead to young people coming to accept the school as a part of their daily lives.

In a detailed analysis of the Youth Training Programme Jean Whyte sets out some lessons for the education service. Whyte uses contemporary evidence from her own work on YTP for NICER and recent evidence from a study carried out by the Public Policy Research Unit to show that some young people leaving school are inadequately prepared for adult working life. Whyte argues that young people are generally disaffected towards school and tend to reject education because of their previous experiences of it. The educational element of YTP therefore had a lot to contend with and presents participants with many challenges in what has become a complex and difficult environment. Whyte indicates that change can only occur when all the educators in the system recognise a need for further modification and variation in education.

In a summative conclusion Leslie Caul argues that education in Northern Ireland is locked into a series of structures that severely limit its potential development. While simultaneously reinforcing testing and assessment the Education Reform Order may generate a new response to continual under-achievement in schools. Whether under-achievement can be alleviated through the Order is open to question.

LESLIE CAUL

PART I

Educational Development or at least leave it as it is

Chapter 1

The Politics of 'No Change'

H. Rex Cathcart
(Professor of Education, Queens University, Belfast)

Introduction

Patterns of control and organisation of schooling in Northern Ireland
are different from those prevailing in the rest of the United Kingdom.
Curricula in the schools have however for some time been similar. So
when it came to implementing the 1988 Education Reform Act in
Northern Ireland the common curriculum was imposed with only
minor modifications, whereas the sections of the Act concerned with
possible changes in the control and organisation of the schools were
largely discarded as irrelevant.

The fate of Westminster educational legislation in Ireland has usually
involved its rejection in part or in whole. British intentions, often in the
past perceived as progressive, especially by Irish teachers' unions, have
been shipwrecked on the rocks of Irish or Northern Irish vested interests. The centres of power and influence in Irish education have simply
resisted pressures to make them conform to the structural forms and
norms of British education. This is almost as true of Protestant bodies,
who presumably have favoured union with Great Britain, as of Catholic
bodies who have not favoured the union. Resistance to conformity in
the curricular field in Northern Ireland has been much less manifest
because the schools have had to maintain equivalent standards to enable
their products to compete in the wider labour markets, and to gain
access to higher and further education, across the Irish Sea.

The history of British educational legislation as applied to Northern
Ireland is revealing for it enables us to establish how British educational policy was reshaped in the province as a means of maintaining
two distinct cultures.

Education in Northern Ireland

From 1930 Northern Ireland has had two parallel sectarian systems of education which have contributed not only to maintaining the distinctions between the two religious groups but have also in large measure ensured the isolation of the groups from one another in the formative years of those who compose them.

The victories of the Protestant clergy in 1925 and 1930 in perverting the non-denominational character of the state schools had a profoundly discriminatory effect. For they meant that a system which received total state subsidisation became Protestant, while the Catholic school system remained only partially subsidised. The 1930 Act implicitly recognised the disparity by attempting to reduce it. From henceforth Catholic schools were to receive 50% grants towards capital costs.

The 1923 Education Act and the amendments which followed it chiefly affected the elementary schools. Very few grammar schools were tempted to enter the orbit of a local authority, although provision was made for them to do so. The organisation and control of the grammar schools remained autonomous as it had been before partition: Protestant schools were run by boards of governors which normally included clerical representation, while Catholic schools were managed by clergy or by religious orders. The schools were recognised by the state if they were not run for profit, in which case their teachers for the most part received state salaries. The schools catered for the privileged minority who could afford their fees, although there was a small-scale state scholarship scheme. The proportion of the Catholic population who received grammar school education was notably smaller than that among Protestants. The grammar schools in both communities had an established, prestigious status, which they have sustained through all the changes which have occurred since the Second World War. In fact, the most remarkable characteristic of post-primary education in Northern Ireland today is the survival of many grammar schools virtually unchanged in control and organisation from the nineteenth century. Their governing bodies have resisted most of the democratising pressures of the age but have, however, been able to take advantage of them to secure their position. Thus, in accepting a larger minority of the age cohort as pupils, they were able to negotiate advantageous terms of expansion. Schools which had pretensions towards the independent public schools, were able to negotiate such terms that there was no temptation to opt out. Perhaps the most significant reason for the success of the governing bodies of the grammar schools is the fact that both the Protestants and the Catholics are united in their determination to preserve this privileged form of schooling.

The Reorganisation of Secondary Education

The governing bodies association was established in response to the imminent implementation by the Northern Ireland government of an equivalent to the 1944 Butler Education Reform Act. There were dimensions of the Act which threatened their freedom. Its intention to ensure that local education authorities used or established schools to suit the talents of all children between the ages of 11 and 15 years carried within it the danger that Northern Ireland grammar schools would be denied the right to select their own pupils. The tripartite system favoured by the Butler Act implied that selection for the grammar schools would be on the basis of tests which singled out the academically able. This would have the effect of denying to the socially suitable but academically unable in Northern Ireland access to grammar school education. Such considerations motivated powerful lobbying of the Stormont government. Its White Paper was reassuring:

> the government are determined that the educational system shall not be inferior to any in the United Kingdom, but to attempt to make it exactly the same as in England and Wales or Scotland would ignore local considerations and deny Ulster the right to shape in their own way what is perhaps the most important of the social services.
>
> (Educational Reconstruction in Northern Ireland)

There was going to be a Northern Ireland interpretation of secondary education for all. The voluntary grammar schools, of which there were 75 as opposed to 9 under the local authorities, were to receive 65% capital expenditure grants in return for conceding 80% of their places to pupils awarded scholarships by the local authorities. The remaining 20% of places would be filled by the grammar schools as they wished. Middle-class parents whose children failed to attain scholarship level could pay their way. This concession drove a 'coach and four' through the principle applied by most local authorities in England and Wales that grammar school intakes should be confined to those selected as academically able. In subsequent years other means emerged whereby the middle class could ensure places for their unqualified children: boarders were not included in quotas and pupils rising from a school's preparatory department and failing to pass the qualifying examination could enter the grammar school and under review, which for some time consisted simply of the principal's word that they could keep up with the rest of the (qualified) class, were awarded scholarships. By such means Northern Ireland's grammar schools sustained their social role as the schools of the middle class. The effect was and is, of course, socially divisive. It is true that in the first year or two after the 1947 Act was passed scholarships were means-tested but this approach was abandoned. It is worthy of note then that the Ministry of Education met the fees charged by the grammar school for each individual scholarship holder. The amount of the fees determined whether they were met in part or in whole. The amount was agreed between the ministry and the governors of the school and allowed for the particular expenses of the school and its traditions. The implications of this concession meant that there could be remarkable disparities between the values of individual scholarships, e.g. in Belfast a boy who attended one school which professed public school status could be subsidised by as much as four times the amount which his sister received from the local authority as her scholarship for attending the nearby girls' grammar school. It took more than 40 years before such inequities became public knowledge as a result of questions in the House of Commons, Westminster, in the autumn of 1988. It should, however, be stated that the aforementioned public school had long since opted out of the category which required it to offer 80% of its places to qualified pupils in return for 65% capital expenditure. It had thus become free for some succeeding years to take as few or as many qualified pupils as it wished.

It was in 1988 too that a legal judgement was made in which the selection procedure for the grammar schools was shown to have passed from the inequitable to the iniquitous from the very beginning. Selection at 11+ had always produced a situation in which a substantially higher proportion of girls passed than of boys. In the circumstances down the years thousands of girls more than boys should have won grammar school scholarships. Instead the Ministry of Education had ruled that in equity the boys' and girls' results should be standardised differently so that equal numbers of boys and girls should get scholarships. Justice Hutton ruled in the High Court, Belfast, on 1 July 1988 that this process of different standardisations constituted direct sex discrimination. The case had been taken to the courts by the Equal Opportunities Commission (NI). Its outcome has historic implications for it must be wondered how many thousands of young girls have over the years been denied access to grammar school education. As we have seen, the means have always existed whereby relatively affluent parents could buy their children into the grammar school system; those who have suffered from the denial therefore have been the girls who came from the social class which could not afford to pay its way.

The alternative to a grammar school for three-quarters of the 11+ age group has been a secondary intermediate school. There was a third possibility in Britain, the technical school, but in Northern Ireland this was scarcely a meaningful one because entrance to a technical intermediate school could only be made after two years at the secondary intermediate. Secondary intermediate schools campaigned to be allowed to provide technical education themselves and were granted the right. The tripartite arrangement was then dropped.

Secondary intermediate schools have never enjoyed parity of esteem with the grammar schools. Conditions from the very beginning made this impossible. In the first place the secondary intermediate system had to be created *ab initio* and in many local authority areas provision for those who were not going on to the grammar schools was very slow in coming. It was not until the 1960s that the county and Catholic authorities had provided a network of purpose built schools. It was not until the mid-sixties that the secondary intermediate schools received anything approaching equal treatment with the grammar schools. Until 1965 there were serious disparities between the teachers' salary scales, staffing ratios, posts of responsibility arrangements, class size and the duration of the school year in the two types of school. All the disparities were of course to the disadvantage of the secondary intermediate schools. The secondary intermediate schools too were frustrated for some time in their efforts to put forward pupils for public examinations. When they became free to do so, they demonstrated that a proportion of their pupils, in spite of institutional constraints, were quite capable of succeeding in academic type examinations.

This fact posed questions about the validity and reliability of the selection process at 11+. Questions had been raised on this score from the beginning and had been referred to the Advisory Council established under the 1947 Act. Indeed they remained the Council's main item of concern for a quarter of a century. The Council recommended various changes in the process from time to time but was slow to reach the conclusion which had been arrived at in Britain, that reorganisation of secondary education on comprehensive lines would obviate the unfairness of selection. There was in fact no strong body of opinion in Northern Ireland in favour of such a reform. This was at least partly attributable to the 'safety valves' which existed enabling middle-class parents to buy the way for their unqualified children into the grammar schools. The strength of the vested interests opposing comprehensivation was, however, never in doubt.

In a remarkable public lecture in 1969, the then permanent secretary

of the Ministry of Education, John Benn, expounded the dire consequences which would follow from comprehensivation:

> To do away with selection in Northern Ireland means the extinc-
> tion of the voluntary grammar schools as they now exist. It means
> also of course the extinction of the 20 or so county grammar
> schools. It means free secondary education all round and the
> handing over to some external authority whether local or central
> of the responsibility for determining what part this or that school
> would play in a new comprehensive system. It means that control
> of entry would have to pass away from the school to a public body,
> local or central. It means of course the end of the grammar school
> preparatory departments as we now know them. It means too I
> think the end of most if not all of the boarding departments as they
> now exist. It means, unless the Government here were to be much
> more ruthless and single-minded than the Government at West-
> minster has yet shown itself to be, that some voluntary grammar
> school, not many perhaps but some, would choose to buy their
> freedom and exist solely as independent fee-charging schools, thus
> creating a far greater social cleavage in the educational system than
> exists today.   (Benn, 1969)

It is astonishing that the danger of two or three voluntary grammar
schools opting for independent status should be perceived as producing greater social cleavage than that already created between the grammar schools and the secondary intermediate schools in Northern Ireland.
This latter is a cleavage, according to one very well informed
commentator, which has contributed far more to maintaining the kind
of society Northern Ireland notoriously has than that between the two
sectarian school systems. It prompted John Malone to go on to say

> The argument those who enjoy the privileges of a selective system
> have to face, is not about whether their children will be better off
> in a non-selective system (indeed many of them might well be bet-
> ter off academically as well in other respects), it is about the kind of
> society they want their children to grow up in.   (Malone, 1988)

In the 1970s while the rest of the United Kingdom 'went comprehensive' until finally some 90% of children were in comprehensive schools,
vested interests in Northern Ireland sought to arrest the tide. It had
become more difficult to marshal effective resistance since direct rule
had replaced the Stormont regime in 1972. The Labour government
under James Callaghan pressed the need for reorganisation of secondary

education in Northern Ireland. The Minister of State with responsibility for education, Lord Melchett, issued a consultative document which indicated the lines on which reorganisation might take place rather than arguing the case for it. The Association of Governing Bodies of Voluntary Grammar Schools became extremely active under its secretary, who happened to have been permanent secretary in one of the important departments of government very recently. It issued a reply to the consultative document which stated *inter alia*: The Association

> believes that the present system of secondary education, developed by evolutionary stages over generations and harnessing as it does the energies and devotion of parents, churches, teachers, statutory boards, former pupils and other friends of the schools, has many valuable features which it would be folly to destroy:

> remembers that whereas it is easy to destroy a living institution, it is hard to rebuild it; places on record the following particular and special characteristics of education in Northern Ireland:

> the absence of independent schools
> the strength and quality of the voluntary grammar schools
> the socially unrestricted opportunity to an all-round academic education which they provide for able children from families with limited means . . .

> believes that by gradual evolution of the best features in the present system it is possible for all children to be educated to the maximum of their individual aptitudes and abilities in conformity with the wishes of their parents (subject only to certain practical limitations); emphasises in harmony with statements in the Universal Declaration of Human Rights, the European Convention on Human Rights and Vatican II on Education that the rights of parents in the education of their children are inalienable and non-negotiable . . .   (AGBVGS in NI, 1977)

Thus Protestant and Catholic authorities came together in a common interest and demanded that the consultative document be withdrawn 'to spare our community needless acrimony and division' (1977).

While the Callaghan government requested local education authorities to go ahead with making plans for reorganisation, it did not press the matter with conviction or determination. It was not a strong government and at the time in Britain reservations about the performance of the educational service were receiving widespread expression, in part stimulated by the Prime Minister himself. The Conservative opposition had by now come to reject outright the policy of comprehensivation. It proposed not simply halting a process which was nearing completion in Britain but reversing it. When the Conservatives came to power in 1979 they immediately indicated that plans for reorganisation should be abandoned and Northern Ireland was included in this. Soon afterwards the government encouraged efforts to reintroduce selection or to extend it where it survived in England. To its surprise such initiatives were firmly opposed by Tory grassroots. This setback helped to prompt the radical reappraisal of the educational system which resulted in the 1988 Reform Act.

Throughout the past decade and more Northern Ireland with its intact bipartite selective system has provided a model for those opposed to comprehensive schools. They point to the steady rise in GCE examination results in Northern Ireland to levels well in excess of those achieved in England and Wales. For example, the percentage of school leavers in Northern Ireland obtaining one or more A levels was 21.1% in 1979-80; 22.3% in 1981-82 and 22.5% in 1983-84. This contrasts with the percentages in England: 14.6% in 1979-80; 17.0% in 1980-81; 17.2% in 1983-84. The other side of this scene has been persistently ignored. The proportion of those leaving school without either GCE or CSE qualifications in Northern Ireland has been consistently more than twice the percentage in England: in Northern Ireland – 27% in 1979-80; 24.3% in 1981-82 and 22.4% in 1983-84. These contrasting extremes in results in Northern Ireland led the head of the Northern Ireland Council for Educational Research to conclude:

> school systems (bipartite in Northern Ireland, comprehensive in England and Wales) by and large achieve what they are expected to achieve. In Northern Ireland's case the selective grammar schools are expected to achieve academic results. Since it is less clear what the secondary schools are expected to achieve one may conclude . . . that they have been left to develop by default.
>
> (Wilson, 1989)

Some 30% of their pupils leave without qualifications; this is not because they have failed in examinations for the most part but because they have not entered for them. The legacy of failure at 11+ often ensures that a sense of inferiority and rejection is sustained to the end of school days. Corrective provision after school in the Northern Ireland Youth Training Programme has little or no effect in improving the job prospects of those without qualifications. They YTP only enhances the prospects of those with five or more 'O' levels (McWhirter, 1989).

It was the bipartite system which produced this range of consequences that enthused the right-wing ideologies and educationalists who provided the rationale for the 1988 Reform Act. It is not surprising that when the Act was extended to Northern Ireland those sections in it which referred to management and control were regarded as inappropriate. In many ways the Northern Irish voluntary grammar school with its autonomy and its substantial control of its own finances is the very model of what the DES hopes to attain with its direct grant schools.

The Educational Reform Order 1989

The new Order imposed a common curriculum on schools and in order to ensure parity for young people in Northern Ireland with those elsewhere in the United Kingdom, it is to be introduced to their schools with only minor modifications. The examination which will explore what has been achieved by sixteen-year-olds in following the common curriculum had already been launched before the Order. The GCSE is a curious misfit in Northern Ireland. It has been devised to test across the full range of ability and so is designed for the comprehensive school. While it is wholly appropriate in Britain, it is somewhat anomalous when applied to the Northern Irish bipartite educational system.

One characteristic of the society which the Conservative government has fostered increasingly in the decade 1979–89 is competition. It is a characteristic which was already manifest in the Northern Ireland educational scene in various ways. Bipartitism ensures that it is a major feature of primary school life, not only between pupils but between schools. Commitment to that competition distorts what the under-elevens do in schools. School inspectors have long recognised that the curriculum is affected by the 11+ tests for selection. In recent years as primary school staffs have sought to implement strategies for school curriculum review, endeavouring thereby to deliver the curriculum more effectively – the project is known as Primary Guidelines – the realisation has grown that preparation for the 11+ is a major impediment to the process. The head of the primary school inspectorate has spoken out strongly against its deleterious effects.

Nevertheless one major purpose of the 1989 Reform Order is to stimulate competition throughout the educational system. The publication of inspectors' reports on schools is now to be followed by the publication of the formal assessments across the common curriculum at the ages of 8, 11, 14 and 16. Teachers will be driven as with the 11+ to concentrate on attaining the highest results to the detriment of the curriculum with its wider purposes. The appearance of league tables of schools' results amounts to the credentialling of schools in a situation where narrow credentialling within schools can already endanger the educational processes.

When competition is promoted in the secondary sector, the effects will undoubtedly be disadvantageous to the secondary intermediate schools. Achievement in output needs to be related to the nature of input in the sense that the levels of ability and aptitude in a school's intake are very relevant to what can be achieved. No provision appears to have been made for the disclosure of this information and so there is no real measure of a school's achievement when it is dealing with pupils who are not in the top quarter to a third of a cohort in terms of academic talent. The die is loaded in publicity terms against the secondary interemediate schools and this will be especially so when other aspects of the Order are implemented.

Open enrolment in a situation of demographic decline means that grammar schools will be advantaged. They may fill all their places without regard to any local education authority's planning arrangements. Parents will simply apply to the school of their preference and the school authorities will select their intake, subject to appeal. As socially ambitious parents have for long shown a strong preference for grammar school places for their children, there will be no enrolment problem for these schools. It is not surprising in the light of their new increased selective powers that under the Order as applied in Northern Ireland all day fees in grammar schools will in future be abolished. The secondary intermediate schools will feel the demographic pinch, even more in the social and academic dimensions than they do already.

Egalitarianism has never been at a premium in education in Northern Irish society. It certainly has become *démodé* in Britain under the Conservative regime 1979–89 and the Reform Order will have the effect of accentuating in Northern Ireland the divisiveness of the educational system, while propagating in time the Northern Irish model in Great Britain.

One distinctive initiative in the Reform Order as applied to Northern Ireland is the return to the promotion of integrated education. British governments favoured such a policy since 1831. It has manifestly been a failure in the teeth of opposition from the clergy. While there is now evidence that there are a number of clergy in the Catholic and Protestant churches who would favour experiments in integrated schooling, there is little doubt that such a development will mainly depend on the breakdown of strict church discipline and the growth of secularisation. There will have to be more à la carte Catholics and Protestants as opposed to those who are table d'hôte members of their churches, accepting the menu as prescribed. Religious conviction, sustained in some measure by the pressures of political alignment, is notoriously strong and inhibits this kind of liberalisation; as a result the conventional British palliative for Irish affairs is destined for modest success. It will not affect either the causes of the 'Troubles' or the participants in and sympathisers with political violence.

Given the fact that the two sectarian school systems will endure, the role which schools can play in diminishing community conflict may be simply stated. It involves the diminution of the isolation between them which has been their main characteristic in the past. The promotion of common projects, social or curricular, shared by linked Protestant and Catholic schools has become an accepted policy of the education authorities. There is another and sometimes related strategy which involves a Northern Irish variant of multi-cultural studies. It is the study of the cultures of the various communities and especially the exploration of the stereotypes and concerns of the community 'on the other side'. Much has been done since the early 1970s to develop education for mutual understanding (EMU). There are however very real limitations to what has been achieved or can be achieved. As a leading pioneer in the field, Alan Robinson, has recently stated:

> The difficulty faced by educators in promoting EMU in schools basically arises from the condition of formal educational institutions themselves. The culture of the school has changed little in Northern Ireland over the last fifteen years and teachers can find that EMU is more effectively undertaken outside school than inside it because ritual is left behind and inter-personal relationships are relaxed. (Robinson, 1988)

The overwhelming emphasis on credentialism in grammar schools has precluded them from including EMU or Irish cultural studies as subjects in their curriculum. Protagonists of the schools have maintained that elements of both subjects have been included in other subjects. As a result of a project in the New University of Ulster, however, a CSE course in (Irish) cultural studies for secondary intermediate schools was available, but these schools will now be required under the Northern Irish version of the 1988 Order to conform to the credentialist pattern and to accept the kind of approach which characterises grammar schools. EMU and Irish Cultural Studies – or cultural heritage, as the subject is now officially designated – are themes which are required to be taught on a cross-curricular basis (DENI, 1988). It remains to be seen whether diffusion equals marginalisation or not. If schools in the secondary sector had been intended to be significant instruments of reconstructionism, Cultural Heritage or EMU would have been a subject in the common curriculum. In its wisdom the Conservative government has decided that this will not be so.

It is an irony that at a time when an initiative had been taken in the secondary sector of Northern Ireland's educational system to promote school-based curriculum review that the government should then proceed in a dirigiste style to tell the schools what their curriculum will be. The 11–16 Programme was designed to stimulate staff in secondary intermediate and grammar schools to become aware of and evaluate the curriculum they were delivering, and to relate it to the needs of the individual pupil and of society. The Programme, like its equivalent in the primary schools – Primary Guidelines, was beginning to win the confidence of teachers and to sensitise them to the ways in which their schools could become more effective. Teachers claimed that '. . . these initiatives would eventually result in the emergence of a broad and balanced curriculum in all schools – in practice a common curriculum' (DENI, 1988). The government was, however, not satisfied with this voluntary participation and decided that it was necessary '. . . to provide in law for a basic curriculum' (DENI, 1988). The 11–16 Programme is to be wound up and the Northern Irish schools have been made to conform to the curricular dimensions of the 1989 Reform Order. To that extent they will be 'normal' within the British context but in most other respects they will continue their existing forms of organisation and control. Eventually, if the Conservative government's intentions are fulfilled, some of these organisations may become normal in Britain.

Chapter 2

The Development of the NICED Primary Guidelines

Sean Vallely
(Director, NICED, Belfast)

Introduction

The process of curriculum review in Northern Ireland primary schools through use of the NICED Primary Guidelines has been ongoing for more than five years. This chapter sets the initiative into its historical context and outlines the thinking at NICED which lay behind the guidelines.

Background

In 1981 a report of a survey which had been undertaken by the Department of Education for Northern Ireland (DENI) inspectorate into primary education in the province stated that the majority of primary schools had no written policies on the curriculum. The survey commented that:

> . . . even when they are available, the curriculum guidelines prepared by principals for their staffs tend to lack clarity and direction . . . much more emphasis should be placed on the development of systematic guidelines within subject areas.   (DENI Inspectorate)

Following the publication of the survey the teacher union representatives on the Standing Conference for Primary Education, having asked DENI to provide appropriate guidelines for primary education, were advised to make an approach to NICED. In response to this approach NICED set up in early 1982 a Primary Programme Committee (PPC) which brought together a number of teachers who had been identified as good classroom practitioners along with a few advisers, college lecturers and members of the inspectorate. The PPC was given the following terms of reference:

> to hold in review the curriculum of primary schools;

in particular to produce guidelines for primary education in Northern Ireland;

to collaborate with other bodies in Northern Ireland concerned with primary education;

to make known developments in primary education elsewhere in the United Kingdom.

Whole curriculum review

Concurrently with the approach from the Standing Conference for Primary Education, NICED had established a small working group to consider issues regarding curriculum review raised in a Schools Council publication 'The Practical Curriculum'. The discussions arising from this publication influenced NICED thinking on the curriculum. A contemporary NICED strategy document indicated an awareness that new approaches to the curriculum were more likely to become embedded in the work of schools if they were in line with the needs and interests of pupils and teachers and that effective curriculum development might best be promoted through whole curriculum review. As a result pilot work was undertaken in whole curriculum review through a number of projects at post primary level and the thinking of the PPC was also influenced by the publications and discussions on whole curriculum review.

Decisions on format

Early discussions at PPC showed that members had a keen appreciation of the holistic approach normally adopted in the primary curriculum and there was considerable debate as to the most appropriate approach to the task of writing guidelines for such a curriculum. While there was a general sympathy with the notion of a single guideline ranging across the whole curriculum this was felt to be an inappropriate format for two very practical reasons; firstly that such a document would be extremely bulky and off-putting to teachers and secondly that writing it would present a very difficult task to PPC members. There was an ensuing debate as to whether an approach through areas of experience might be appropriate (e.g. subsuming history, geography and science within environmental studies and music, art and design, physical education and drama within creative and aesthetic studies) but in the event a decision was made in favour of single subject guidelines with cross-curricular references being introduced in each wherever possible.

Nine subjects for which guidelines would be produced were identified as follows:

music
science
mathematics
health and social education
language and literacy
physical education
art and design
history
geography

The 9 Curricular Guidelines were intended to facilitate curriculum review by promoting staff discussion on each particular aspect of the curriculum along the following lines:

What is meant by this aspect of the curriculum within the primary school/within our primary school?

What benefits might accrue to an individual child in terms of the development of attitudes, values, concepts and qualities as well as knowledge and skills?

How might it be taught?

What resources and support are available to the teacher?

It was agreed that the guidelines would be addressed initially to principals and that an Introductory Booklet would be produced to support principals in working with the whole staffs to institute review and to develop statements of school policy and aims.

Support for dissemination and implementation

From the outset NICED recognised the importance of ensuring support for implementation of the guidelines at school level. Since the experiences of former bodies indicated that curriculum development 'by post' did not work there would have been little point in sending guideline copies to schools unless proper groundwork had been carried out and continuing support was available. This point had been confirmed in recommendations contained in a report by NICER into the uptake in primary schools of initiatives supported by the previous Northern Ireland Schools Curriculum Committee,

> . . . NICED must take cognisance of what has been learned in recent years about the management of innovation in schools . . . and try to ensure that future schemes are adequately planned and served . . . only by bringing help and support to teachers in their schools is there hope of bringing about real change in the curriculum.
>
> (Sutherland, 1981)

While NICED's general remit from DENI was 'to be responsible for initiating, supporting and co-ordinating activities in curriculum development and associated educational technology which have implications for schools and institutions of further education in Northern Ireland', it was not intended that this remit should extend beyond pilot work aimed at developing new approaches and the offering of advice. NICED never contemplated, nor was it staffed to undertake, the implementation of major curriculum exercises. Before starting guideline production, therefore, it was necessary to ensure that support at school level would be forthcoming and, with this in mind, NICED entered into discussions with the many partners who would become involved in the implementation exercise. These partners included the ELBs which were pleased to undertake the major exercise of implementation; DENI which agreed to provide funds to support the exercise and, in particular, to fund the provision of substitute teacher cover during in-service developmental work; the Governing Bodies Association, the maintained school authorities and the teacher unions, all of which gave their backing to the exercise; and the teacher education institutions, which agreed to help in the provision of in-service support for the implementation exercise where appropriate.

Phasing

It was decided that the release of the guidelines would be phased over a number of years so that schools would not be overwhelmed by the level of change that might be required. Since there was a perceived tradition of concentration in Northern Ireland schools on the 3 Rs it was felt best that the mathematics and English (language and literacy) booklets should be held back somewhat to avoid reinforcing this tradition. The Introductory Booklet was to be accompanied at its launch by one of the subject guidelines which would illustrate the review process and which schools could use as an exemplar for initial work. The Health and Social Education Guideline was selected for this purpose since it addressed a curricular area which was not widely developed in primary schools but was one which NICED felt should be included in the entitlement of all pupils. There was some surprise expressed in schools that this guideline should be the first to appear, especially since there had appeared to be little demand from teachers for it. In the event, a reasonable cohort of schools fairly quickly came to appreciate its appropriateness and the close way in which it integrated with the Introductory Booklet, and took up review and development in this curricular area as a priority. Release of the guidelines thereafter related mainly to their availability at the end of what became a fairly arduous process for staff at NICED of writing, revision and editing.

Support papers

From the outset, the guidelines publications were regarded by PPC as falling into three categories:

> an introductory booklet to encourage principals to consider undertaking review. Since many principals had no great experience of review it raised questions about the purposes of primary education within the context of what each school was currently doing;

> the further nine booklets in the series, dealing with key aspects of the curriculum;

> a series of mainly short support papers arising from the needs and experiences of schools undertaking review. These papers would address a wide range of organisational, administrative and procedural issues, not all of which would be of direct interest to every school.

In autumn 1983 PPC identified the following as possible topics to be addressed in short support papers:

> the small rural school
> parents and the school
> self-evaluation of the school
> staff development
> continuity in the curriculum
> inter-school links
> the role of the head
> the role of the co-ordinator
> children with special needs
> the use of the media

the curriculum for the four year-old child
topic work
cross-curricularity
homework
marking children's work
curriculum balance
discipline
record-keeping
microtechnology in the primary school
materials evaluation
display in the classroom
classroom management
the structuring of play
selecting reading schemes
note-making

It was agreed that priority should be given to the guidelines series and that drafting of support papers should take place when time permitted. In autumn 1986 the list of topics for the short papers was considered, amended and prioritised and the first paper to be published was:

The Curriculum for the Four Year Old Child in the Primary School (autumn 1988).

This was followed in 1989 by:

The Role of the Principal in Review and Development
Classroom Management/Organisation
A School Homework Policy
Introducing IT in the Primary School
The Small School

Other topics in preparation during 1988/89 were:

Parents and the School
Children with Special Needs
Evaluating Children's Work

Evaluation

The widespread uptake by primary schools across the province indicates to what extent teachers perceived the guidelines as a useful framework for curriculum development. Principals pointed out that an increasing collegiality among staff led to schools becoming more cohesive units. It remains very difficult, however, to assess to what extent the aims and objectives outlined in school policy statements have been implemented in classrooms or review of individual subject areas has led to worthwhile curriculum development.

In early 1986 the Northern Ireland Council for Educational Research (NICER) conducted an appraisal of the first stages of the review and development of the language programmes in some Belfast schools which used the Language and Literacy Guideline. The views of principals, co-ordinators and class teachers were obtained through interviews and questionnaires and the findings published. The final report illustrated the concerns, anxieties and uncertainties which an exercise in review provokes, as well as the general acceptance of the need for such an exercise and the intention of schools to take on more guidelines in future years. It also indicates that there is an ongoing need for support if this curriculum initiative, welcomed as it was by principals and teachers, is to continue to succeed. In particular, the report identifies the need for continuing INSET support, time for the process of review, expert support services and funding for classroom resources.

No comprehensive survey has, as yet, been undertaken of the outcomes, benefits and lessons to be learnt as a result of what has been the largest exercise in review ever undertaken in Northern Ireland. The way ahead in curriculum review and development would be usefully illuminated by a more comprehensive appraisal of the work arising from the NICED Primary Guidelines.

Conclusion

This chapter has attempted to set the Primary Guidelines initiative in its historical context and to outline its development as a learning process for all the partners in the exercise – schools, ELBs, NICED and other bodies involved. In retrospect it will probably be perceived as a worthwhile element in the organic growth of education in Northern Ireland. It certainly had a major impact on thinking about the primary curriculum and the influence of the publications has extended beyond the province especially since they became commercially available in other parts of the UK through publication by Longman. Of course all curriculum initiatives have now been overtaken by decisions of the government on the reform of education. There would appear to be a continuing place, however, within the new curriculum arrangements for the approaches and outcomes of the guidelines initiative.

The Government fully recognises the contribution of Primary Guidelines . . . to the development of a coherent approach to curriculum organisation . . . The progress which (this) initiative has made . . . has contributed significantly to curriculum thinking in the participating schools, and in many this is already being reflected in the quality of their educational provision . . . the Government is also determined to take account of the valuable lessons which have been learnt in curriculum initiatives in Northern Ireland and to build on these in the development and implementation of the common curriculum.

(DENI 1988, The Way Foward)

Chapter 3

A Programme of Curriculum Review and Development in Secondary Schools

Anne O'Shea
(Director, 11–16 Programme, Belfast)

Secondary Education Today

Too much is expected of our secondary schools and little is provided to support them in the tasks they are asked to perform. The sheer size of some schools, the multitude of tasks and the need to co-ordinate the range of teaching activities provided requires a very complicated system of organisation and communication.

Aims, Goals and Expected Outcome of the 11–16 Programme

Secondary schools can tend to treat young people as if they were disembodied minds, desensitised containers to be filled with knowledge. Psychologists, however, have long since argued that the most important task for the adolescent is to establish an adult identity and to be seen to be capable of taking responsibility. Is the organisation of the secondary school conducive to the facilitation of learning and the development of the maturing young person? Is the way in which we teach and, to some extent, what is taught too frequently unhelpful in the education of young people? The explosion of development that occurs at adolescence creates new and exciting opportunities for learning. Intelligence attains its maximum capacity, physical development is greatly enhanced, sexual differentiation is emphasised and aesthetic sensitivity is sharpened. Individual identity has to be searched for and all the problems relating to others sorted out. Passing academic exams was not a good substitute for learning to be an adult. In a society where there are few jobs and a significant number of young people leave school without even a single certificate of competence, curricular change was a necessity.

The 11–16 Programme was publicly launched in February 1984 and its main aim was stated as follows:

to improve the quality and relevance of education for all pupils in the age-range 11–16 but particularly for those young people who do not relate positively to secondary education and who currently achieve little from it.   (11–16 Programme, 1984)

The objectives for the Programme were set out in the following order: to effect a programme of review and development work in the educational provision for 11–16 year-olds, with the object of achieving:

an agreed policy for educational provision within schools

a redesigned curriculum

changes in the classroom in both content and approach to learning

an appropriate assessment procedure for these pupils which is understood and valued by parents, other agencies and the world of work

a teaching force with appropriate training

ample ranges of teaching/learning materials

a support structure of experienced, senior personnel to advise, assist and work with the staff in each school

a balanced range of contact and work with parents, other schools, other educational, social and economic agencies including the Youth Service, commerce and industry.

In summary, the Programme would aim to achieve significant change in the organisation of teaching and learning, both inside and beyond the classroom, from all pupils, irrespective of ability. It would also aim to provide additional support and enhanced professional satisfaction for teachers.

The Philosophy of the 11–16 Programme

The most significant aspect of the 11–16 Programme was that unlike other local educational initiatives, it was not directed at one dimension of school life but at all aspects of schooling. Its primary focus was the review and development of the curriculum of secondary schools.

Another important feature of the Programme was that it was focused on the individual school and took account of individual distinctive features – location, staffing, enrolment, organisation, culture, aims and objectives. It was primarily directed towards helping schools to meet the requirement that all young people, whatever their ability or talent, should have access to a broad, relevant, balanced, differentiated and challenging curriculum.

With regard to the rapid changes in society and more particularly in education, the 11–16 Programme intended to help schools adapt in a constructive and meaningful manner without sacrificing the tradition and local standing of the institution. By encouraging teachers to identify issues for review and development as well as to manage the exercise in their own schools it was hoped to initiate a continuing process. This implied a need for a systematic and thorough review which would be sustained for a considerable period of time.

Such a process would require organisational as well as curricular change. It would demand changes in timetabling, in decision-making procedures, in management structures, in modes of communication, in teaching methods and classroom organisation, in assessment and guidance procedures, in relationships between staff as well as between staff and pupils. In fact, it would encompass the whole gamut of activities and processes which constitute the institutions we recognise as schools. Change on such a scale would not happen without a willingness on the part of all concerned to learn new concepts, processes and skills. The most important of these skills were those of problem-solving:

a) diagnosis of the present situation;
b) search for and invention of solutions and resources;
c) mobilisation of actions to make these solutions a reality;
d) steady monitoring of progess as it happens;
e) taking corrective action if the future does not look like what was envisaged.

All of these activities presuppose a clear vision on the part of all concerned of where they wished the school to go; above all, it demanded the will to get there and the commitment of the entire staff to the achievement of these goals.

Strategies and Means

This was a regional programme of curriculum review and development. On a macro level it was intended to affect the whole secondary school sector including the various support agencies. On a micro level the focus of the programme was narrowed to individual classrooms and teachers. It was envisaged that all secondary (including grammar) schools would have the opportunity to join the Programme over a period of five to seven years. For ease of administration it was decided that ten schools in each of the five Board areas would join the Programme in the first year. Schools were invited to 'contract in' to the programme and to indicate their commitment to educational development by setting out their priorities for change. They were also expected to commit a minimum weekly allocation of time to the Programme and to select an internal co-ordinator and committee to oversee the work of review and development in the school. This committee would also liaise with external support personnel. It was intended that similar procedures would obtain in subsequent years with regard to entry to the Programme, though the actual number of schools which enrolled in the Programme in any year might be affected by factors such as the pace of development work in progress, the absence of industrial action by teachers and the capacity of the Programme's support personnel in each of the five areas.

Resources

The main responsibility for support within each Board area was devolved to a member of the Inspectorate of the Department of Education and a Board Officer. Field Officers (who are seconded teachers) were also engaged to act as school support personnel in each area. They worked as members of an area team with the designated Inspector and Board Officer. One or more members of this team attended the weekly meeting in each of the schools to support each school committee. It was the school committee that decided on procedures for review, conducted the initial surveys and consultations and collated the findings. This committee was also charged with the task of engaging heads of subject departments in the review and development process and it was expected that the committee would be constantly involved in consultation with the principal and staff to keep the Programme rolling. In all of these tasks the schools were supported by members of the area team of Programme personnel. The role of these teams was to facilitate the work of the curriculum committee by asking significant questions, suggesting appropriate modes of action, coming up with alternative ideas, organising in-service training both on and off-site and generally supporting the school with resources when they were required.

Each school was guaranteed access to support for a period of five years. In each of the five years a sum of between £5000-£10 000 was made available over and above normal financial provision. This money was intended for use by schools to enhance curricular provision for all pupils and it could not be diverted to other purposes. The area team acted as a monitoring body for the appropriate use of resources. The money was generally used for equipment, books, residential experiences out of school, reprographics, theatre visits, field trips, historical outings. It could also be used to purchase ancillary staff time but not teaching staff time.

In-service Training

Perhaps the most important resource to which schools had access through the Programme was in-service training both on and off school sites. Substitute teachers were available to schools to enable groups of staff to meet for discussion and development of the curriculum. Substitute teacher allocation was initially on a ratio of one substitute teacher per staff member per year, thus giving a school of 47 teachers 47 substitute teacher days. These could be used in any combination facilitating the release from teaching duties of groups of staff for half or whole day meetings as well as for other forms of in-service training, tailored to particular roles and tasks, which was provided, as required, mainly by the external support team. A one-day closure was also available to each school per year to be used as and when it was considered appropriate by the co-ordinating committee. Five extra 'closures' were included as a normal part of the school year in the fourth year of the Programme's existence.

Information

Information resources were also available to schools through a variety of sources. The external support team acted as an imporant channel-and-filter in this respect by keeping the co-ordinating committee informed on useful reading matter. Members of the team prepared materials for schools which offered ideas and models for operation based on good practice elsewhere, thus saving time and giving teachers the reassurance that models were based on successful experience in other programmes. Reading lists were regularly updated and useful information circulated to schools.

Co-ordination

The 11–16 Programme was co-ordinated at a regional level by a Regional Co-ordinator, whose main tasks were designated as follows by the Department of Education:

> The Regional Co-ordinator will be responsible to the programme's Regional Consultative Committee and will work with the team of Inspectors and Board Officers assigned to the Programme. He/She will have responsibility for:
>
> (a) Advising the Regional Consultative Committee about the nature and scope of particular initiatives.
> (b) Co-ordinating the activity of the Inspectorate/Board team.
> (c) Establishing contacts and communication among the participating schools.
> (d) Maintaining close liaison with related initiatives such as the Transition to Adult and Working Life (TRAWL) Project, Secondary Science Curriculum Review, Fourth and Fifth Year Curriculum Project.
> (e) Dissemination of the work undertaken by individual schools and groups of schools.
> (f) Establishing close working links between the programme and the Centre for Educational Management.
> (g) Advising on suitable methods of informing parents, employers and others about the work of the programme.

The Programme for the participating schools is intended to cover two main phases:

> 1. Appraisal of each school's existing curriculum against the current aims of the school.
> 2. Discussion and review of these aims and practices against an acceptable framework of desirable practice for the future and action to implement consequential changes in content and approach.

> Members of the Programme team — Inspectorate and Board Officers — would work with the curriculum groups in each participating school during both phases, giving professional help through discussion, preparation of materials and working with teachers where appropriate. The Regional Co-ordinator would, in liaison with members of the team encourage the development of innovative work in the curriculum and would establish close con-

tacts with teacher-training institutions in an attempt to promote a co-ordinated approach to necessary in-service training provision.

The Regional Co-ordinator reported on a regular basis to a Regional Consultative Committee which was responsible for advising on the policy and direction of the Programme. This committee was broadly based, representative of all those bodies who had some responsibility for the oversight of secondary education throughout Northern Ireland. The committee usually met once per term but extraordinary meetings were called at other times as the need arose.

Evaluation

In general the first two years in the Programme were spent in laying solid foundations through review of existing curricular provision. Such an exercise gradually spread throughout the school to become, in time, a whole school activity. Cross-curricular issues such as assessment or the development of active learning approaches or study skills were promoted in conjunction with the development of units of work. The nett effect of this broad range of review and development work has been that in many schools there has been a considerable improvement in the quality of pupils' classroom experiences, and an enhancement of the acquisition skills and concepts within more enjoyable learning experiences. Such work is slow and time-consuming and is frequently extra to the work of a normal teaching day. The following range of activities have featured in the development work carried out in various schools:

Study, learning and communication skills
Active or participative learning experiences in a wide range of subjects
Personal and social education (including health education)
Economic awareness
Science offered to many more pupils
Technology offered to more pupils including girls
Adult and working-life modules integrated with normal curriculum
Development of records of achievement.

Other elements such as child care, media education, information technology, outdoor pursuits and design activities added breadth and balance to the curriculum of other year groups in some schools. There is no uniform pattern. Much of this work was supported and given considerable impetus by GCSE or the introduction of B/Tec/CGLI 14-16 pre-vocational work. This new emphasis on assessment will be given further fillip by the proposals for a common curriculum with in-built attainment targets and standard attainment tasks already being devised to measure progress.

A Common Curriculum

The shape of things to come in Northern Ireland has already been out-lined in 'The Way Forward' (DENI, 1988). The 11–16 Programme has been overtaken by events and schools will no longer be able to deter-mine for themselves what their curriculum for different year groups should be. One of the main features of the 'The Way Forward' is a com-mon curriculum framework consisting of six essential areas of study to be offered by all schools, both primary and secondary. Schools, which have been working for some years with the support of the 11–16 Pro-gramme Team should find themselves well placed to undertake the range of work which will still be required for the implementation of a common curriculum. The processes of curriculum design and delivery have always been at the heart of Programme activities. These processes will be even more necessary in the future, as school get to grips with the recommendations of the working groups. It will still be up to each school to work out for itself the best ways of delivering the common curriculum, given the normal constraints on time, personnel and accommodation. Those processes have already been set in train in most 'Programme' schools and are well developed in many of them. A further important legacy of the 11–16 Programme will be the internal structures of curricular deliberation and decision-making, which were established as part of the Programme Team's contract with schools. These structures may need to be altered or fine-tuned to meet future demands, but the essential framework for decision-making is already in place.

Chapter 4

The TRAWL Project 1983–87: Assumptions, Intentions and Effects

Peter P. Daws

(Dean of Education and Director TRAWL, University of Ulster)

Introduction

The Transition to Adult Working Life (TRAWL) Project 1983–87 has been unique in Northern Ireland in being part of a wider European Community programme of 30 similar projects across 10 countries, thus providing access to a rich source of ideas and perspectives on aims and related curriculum developments, 14-18 year-olds. The 16 post-primary schools in the project benefited. As well as generating a con-siderable amount of promising innovation designed to address the requirements of effective and responsible citizenship alongside the pursuit of scholarship, it has wrought a revolution in the professional practice of post-primary teachers by replacing fragmented, indepen-dent subject teaching with corporate planning and delivery of the total curriculum.

The project was unique among EC projects in including a 'consumer' dimension: fifth-form pupils were assessed on a range of life-related areas of understanding and competence, and their views sought on their needs and the adequacy of their school experience in meeting those needs. They were also re-interviewed at one and two-year inter-vals post-school leaving.

The work of TRAWL in updating the post-primary curriculum has been taken forward through later projects, notably the 11–16 Curricu-lum Project and the Vocational Educational Project (Northern Ireland's alternative to TVEI) and helped to shape NICED thinking on the 11–16 Curriculum (NICED, 1986).

Some identified structural deficiencies remain. Because of the inher-ent competition among agencies – schools, colleges and the Youth Training Programme – for young people post-16, full information on opportunities for continued education and training is still unavailable to many young people in their final year of compulsory schooling, and the guidance available to them is too often far from disinterested. In addition, discontinuities of curriculum philosophy, purpose and provision remain between what is provided pre-16 and post-16. The proposed National Curriculum for Northern Ireland, though the TRAWL Project experience has clearly contributed to its shape, in, for example, its grouping of subjects into areas of study and the prominence it gives to cross-curricular themes, stops short at 16 and fails to address the entry requirements of those programmes that begin at 16, both inside and outside schools.

European influences

In 1976, concurrently with the initiation in Britain of the 'Great Debate', the European Parliament for the first time voted funds for educational purposes, to finance projects across the member states designed to 'assist policy formation, 14-18' in relation to the vocational preparation of young people. The results of those projects, which occupied the years 1977–81, were sufficiently encouraging to justify the launch of a second 'transition' programme of 30 projects across the 10 member states, 1983–87. One of these was the TRAWL (Transition to Adult and Working Life) Project.

It was recognised by the Council of Ministers, which endorsed the programmes, that the pace of change, post-war, in Western Europe had been so rapid that educational systems had been unable to keep pace. Innovative correction was needed, in particular, in relation to:

occupational change, notably in the content and structure of the labour market and the skill mix required;

in increased sophistication of technological, bureaucratic and economic processes of people's daily lives;

in the values that regulated social life, notably the pluralistic, multi-cultural basis of European life and the concern to eliminate all forms of discrimination, including gender discrimination; and

a heightened need to prepare young people to participate in an informed way in political and community debate and to contribute constructively to democratic processes at all levels.

In addition to these commonly agreed priorities, the projects in the second 'transition' programme began with a (non-prescriptive) agenda of specific professional matters which the experience of the first programme had revealed as worthy of attention. They may be summarised as follows:

disadvantaged groups
ethnic minorities
low achievers and 'drop outs'
girls and young women

educational structures
links between schooling and vocational training
guidance and information systems

curriculum content
the new technologies, e.g. work experience
use of out-of-school personnel
cross-curricular group project work, e.g. mini companies

assessment and accreditation
profiling and profiles
records of achievement
oral methods

staff development
prompt ways of supportively responding to teachers and schools
involved in innovation.

One additional political value emerged and gathered strength during the decade spanned by the two programmes: the need to imbrue young people with a sense of their common European heritage, and to develop in addition to their sense of their separate national identities, that of being a citizen of Europe, which became reflected in a variety of curriculum initiatives. In the mid-1970s, one talked of the European Commission; by the mid-1980s, the term 'European Community' was firmly in place – at least, in mainland Europe.

The TRAWL team of field workers, all seconded teachers, were supported in their work by a team of European project co-ordinators based in Cologne. They had ready access to colleagues in 29 other projects in 10 member states, incuding GB and Eire, regular inter-project visits to exchange experiences and theme-based workshops and conferences in Europe. The value of having in Northern Ireland, for once, a curriculum development initiative that was infused with a wider framework of reference and a much more extended source of ideas cannot be over-emphasised. The TRAWL team and the teacher teams in the sixteen participating schools found the stimulation of a wide-ranging flow of ideas from such a variety of sources particularly refreshing and enriching. Entrenched ideas and traditional practices were subject to searching challenge.

TRAWL: curriculum development

The project's purpose was:

> to examine the extent to which post-primary schools prepare young people for the practical demands and responsibilities that life will pose for them in the years following their compulsory schooling;

> to note curriculum inadequacies in relation to identified need and help the project schools plan and implement appropriate curriculum and curriculum-related change;

> to develop models of good practice that could be recommended for dissemination and adoption by other post-primary schools.

A representative sample of sixteen volunteer schools was selected to provide a geographical spread across the five Education and Library Boards (ELBs) and a balance of secondary intermediate and grammar schools, urban and rural, controlled and maintained (in effect, Protestant and Catholic schools), single-sex and mixed and one special school.

As a result of research into the conditions of viability and adoption of curriculum development projects, in England (Steadman *et al*, 1981) and in Northern Ireland (Sutherland, 1981, Sutherland *et al*, 1983), it was decided that a non-prescriptive but supportive, serving relationship should be developed by the project team towards the participating schools, to foster a within-school sense of project ownership, control and responsibility. Only one requirement was imposed: each school should conduct a whole-school curriculum review, that is, each should examine its entire curriculum in respect of its contribution to equipping its statutory school-leavers to cope with social and occupational demands and responsibilities, post-16, and that all levels of the teaching staff should be involved to some degree in the conduct of the review and should understand its purpose. A variety of instruments was prepared at the schools' request by the project team (questionnaires, checklists, etc.) to aid them in this curriculum analysis. The project team, which was recruited in the spring of 1983, consisted of a part-time director and three full-time field officers who were seconded teachers; a fourth was added in 1984. All had had some successful experience of curriculum development. They visited the schools regularly, participated in school project team discussions, responded to requests for material and provided relevant papers, ideas, etc. A classified list of curriculum areas and issues that merited consideration is provided in Table 4.1.

The list was not given to the schools, partly because it is too dauntingly ambitious and partly because it may have been perceived as an undisclosed target or hidden agenda. Rather, it was the project team's comprehensive range of matters worthy of consideration of which any school, however ambitious, could address only a small sample in the time available.

One by one, schools came to see their task as that of devising a relevant curriculum, and therefore of adding the claims of citizenship to those of scholarship, yet each school had to recognise that since the time available for teaching/learning remained unaltered, little headway could be made by simply adding new courses. The more interesting aspect of the schools' thinking eventual achievement lay in the variety of answers they found to this problem, which required the achievement of increased learning and the concurrency of a greater multiplicity of learning outcomes per unit of time, the crucial variables for manipulation being:

> the pupils' motivation, engagement and ability in relation to learning tasks;

> the teachers' commitment, organisation skill in patterning objectives and capacity to identify and respond to the needs of individual pupils;

> the range of teaching methods available to be invoked as appropriate;

> the concurrent organisation of those learning tasks that can be addressed simultaneously, perhaps conventionally dispersed across different areas of the curriculum; and

> the optimum sequencing of learning experiences.

On the basis of their completed reviews and strongly influenced by the findings of the TRAWL school-leaver research (which is outlined in the following section), a wide variety of developments was embarked upon across the sixteen schools, prominent among them being:

1. Personal and Social Education, notably
   communication, oral and written
   self -presentation, negotiation and transaction skills.
2. **Personal and Family Matters**

Table 4.1 Trawl Evaluation Schedule

A Social & personal education	B Careers education	C Enterprise education	D Moral education for democratic citizenship	E Numeracy, science & technology	F Gender education & gender equality
(a) How Society Works (b) Money Management (c) Communication (d) Health Education (e) Consumer Education (f) Study Skills (g) Personal Relationships (h) Decision-Making (i) Parenthood & Family Life (j) Political Education (k) Personal Qualities	(a) Self-Awareness (b) Opportunity Awareness (c) Work Experience (d) Decision-Making (e) Leisure Education (f) Pre-Vocational Courses	(a) Self-Esteem (b) Survival Skills (c) Productive Skills (d) Self-Employment (e) Problem-Solving (f) Autonomy	(a) Understanding & Tolerance (b) Compassionate Concern for Disadvantaged (c) Ecological Education (d) World Issues (e) Human Rights (f) European Citizenship (g) Value Formation	(a) Science & Everyday Life (b) Measurement & Calculation (c) Data Education (d) Girls & Science Curriculum (e) Curriculum Up-Dating (f) Computer Education (g) Information Technology & Teaching Methods	(a) Gender Education (b) Gender Bias in Educational Material (c) Equality of Curriculum Access (d) Gender Equality & Guidance

G Pastoral care, guidance & information	H Community involvement	I Pupil categorisation	J Assessment & certification	K Organisation & management	L Staff development
(a) Induction Programmes (b) Yr 3 Option Choice (c) Post-16 Guidance (d) Pupils at Risk (e) Remedial Strategies (f) Discipline (g) Pastoral Care	(a) Out-of-School Learning (b) School Policy (c) In-School Learning (d) Home & School (e) Employers (f) Feeder Primary Schools (g) FE & HE (h) Health & Social Services (i) Shared Teaching with Other Schools	Age Sex Ability Uncontrollable Remedial Need Handicap Disadvantaged Religion Ethnicity etc.	(a) Pupil Records (b) Profiles & Profiling (c) Records of Achievement	(a) School Structures (b) Self-Monitoring & Self-Evaluation System	(a) School Policy & Practice (b) Identified Need

health
parenthood
consumer education
3. Economic Awareness
practical/applied mathematics
money management
economic understanding
4. 'Technics'
practical manual skills
tools and equipment
wiring circuits, fuses, etc.
technology and design
information technology
5. Enterprise Education
mini-enterprise projects
scientific problem-solving projects
pre-vocational studies
6. Community Involvement
liaison with industry, colleges of further education, the Youth
Training Programme
parental involvement
out-of-school learning, e.g. work experience
use of out-of-school personnel to contribute to in-school as well as
out-of-school programmes
7. Vocational Guidance
improved information
more help to formulate and implement plans
8. Assessment and Accreditation
broadening the range of recognised achievement
extending the range of modes of assessment
curriculum negotiation
profiling and profiles
records of achievement
computerised pupil record systems

More impressive than this list of curriculum initiatives and of more
significance for the future practice of school teaching has been the shift
from professional isolation and independence of practice to habits
of collective debate about the purposes of the whole curriculum,
corporate planning and co-operation in teaching. Post primary school
teachers are unaccustomed to being asked to reflect upon the total

product, boy or girl, or to formulate views about what might be operationally implied by such curriculum design principles as balance or breadth, coherence and relevance of progression. Their involvement in a whole-school curriculum review required that they address such global curricular issues. Furthermore, having to face that much of the additional learning to be achieved is not 'owned' by any one familiar subject and cannot, because of constraints of time, be merely added as a 'new' subject and must, therefore, be distributed in a manner that makes logical and psychological sense across a range of subjects requires teachers to co-operate across subject boundaries in orchestrating their contributions to achieve common ends. This shift of professional stance from fragmented independence of contribution to corporate planning and delivery is difficult and courageous but was achieved by many teachers in the TRAWL schools in a period when morale among teachers had rarely been so low. It has profound implications for curriculum design and modes of delivery. In exploring the notion of cross-curricularity as an appropriate way of distributing responsibility for added dimensions of learning, the TRAWL project team and the schools were helped by HM Inspectorate's notion of areas of experience to which all pupils have a right of access (DES, 1978).

TRAWL: consumer research

Pupils in their final year of compulsory schooling in the project schools were tested to determine their knowledge and competence in a range of matters relevant to street sense and worldly wisdom. Also, samples of such pupils were taken in consecutive years (1984 and 1985) and inter-viewed in depth about their post-school ambitions and asked to rate a range of life-related accomplishments in terms of their importance for life, their sense of personal preparedness and the adequacy of the help they had received from their schools. These samples were followed up and re-interviewed at one year and at two years after finishing their period of obligatory schooling.

Knowledge of school-leaver competence and of the ways they perceived the world's requirements of them and their own needs con-stituted valuable bench-mark data that revealed the size and detail of the task confronting schools. For this reason, the schools welcomed it. In large measure, it confirmed the teachers' own judgement of what needed to be done and enabled them to feel some confidence in their judgement. But there were also some valuable surprises.

a. The Cohort Assessment Programme

The entire final compulsory year population in 15 schools (N=1569) completed a 2½ hour battery of tests in the winter of 84/85, covering many areas of knowledge and competence related to the requirement. The time available was too short to permit more than a limited sampling of their capabilities. We concentrated on essential minimal competences and knowledge that should have elicited a 95% success rate (except for certain standardised tests marked*):

> basic arithmetical competence*
> reading for retention and understanding
> social competence and self-esteem*
> general and social knowledge in the areas of:
> > education and training opportunities, post-16
> > money management
> > consumer knowledge
> > economic awareness
> > political knowledge
> > personal health and health-related behaviour
> > knowledge of local facilities
> practical and household knowledge
> self-presentation (completing a job application form).

Results showed a large number of pupils, including many of high ability, lacked much that is needed to conduct efficiently the ordinary business of daily life. One finds the physics student with an inadequate knowledge of basic tools and electrical wiring, the arts student who completes an application form badly and many who cannot apply simple arithmetic to undemanding household tasks. The numeracy test confirmed the DES/APU data (DES, 1980) that, by UK standards, we have a good proportion of high-fliers but a long tail of hardly-numerates: 24% of our sample obtained an arithmetical age score of 12 years or less.

Awareness of further education and training courses available to them outside of school, particularly of the Youth Training Programme, was unexpectedly and disturbingly poor. Young people appear to know where they want to go, occupationally speaking, but are ill-informed about access routes and probabilities of arrival. They revealed a similarly poor awareness of economic and financial management matters, and of safe ways of handling domestic tools and appliances. Health knowledge was impressive on smoking and solvent abuse but less so on general rules of health and hygiene.

Particularly revealing were their efforts to complete a job application form. It was devised to reflect the requirement of many forms regularly used in Northern Ireland, and when completed, was assessed for us by personnel for the NI Electricity Service, who marked them for content and presentation, each on a five-point scale. Only 29% of the pupils achieved one of the top two grades on both content and presentation, and these comprised 13% of the boys and 42% of the girls! Even allowing for a few more bright girls than boys in the sample, the extent of this difference is startling.

A sample of the bleaker findings from this programme is provided in Table 4.2.

b. The Case Study Programme

Samples of final compulsory year pupils were drawn from the project schools, 72 in each year, 1984 and 1985. Each school was asked to provide three pupils (six in mixed sex schools) selected by the following criteria:

> likely to make a good adjustment to adult and working life;
> likely to make an average adjustment to adult and working life;
> likely to have difficulty in adjusting to adult and working life.

Interviewers were not told the category into which the children were placed and no child was interviewed by a teacher from his/her own school. The purpose of the structured interview was to determine their immediate and longer-term ambitions, their knowledge of education and training courses available to them at 16+ and their judgements in relation to a range of areas of knowledge, communication skills and personal qualities of:

(a) their importance for coping with the demands of adult life,
(b) how well they felt personally prepared to meet those demands, and
(c) the adequacy with which their schools had tried to help them acquire these things.

The main findings have been summarised in Tables 4.3–4.7.

The pupils showed a major preoccupation with employment prospects and requirements, but they revealed also an awareness of the demands that will be made upon them as consumers, homebuilders, spouses and parents as well as workers. However, they take a very practical view of adult life's demands and have much less sense of their

Table 4.2   *What Many School-Leavers did not know/could not do (N=1569) (Percentages represent SLs who did not know/could not do)*

Divide 600 in the ratio 3:2:1	74%
Express 17/1000 as a decimal fraction	65%
Interpret a simple histogram (bar graph)	43%
Show any awareness of YTP or the Local Enterprise Development Unit (LEDU)	39%
Practical Domestic Knowledge:	
use a plumb line	44%
wire a plug	43%
purpose of a fuse	89%
Money Matters:	
Sale of Goods Act	67%
ownership & hire purchase	40%
insurance premium	34%
Complete a job application form to a good standard	71%
No. of member states in the European Community	70%

Table 4.3   *Importance for Life: (a) School-leavers' top ten ratings*

1.	Responsibility and Trustworthiness	277
2.	Knowledge of employment and training opportunities, post-16	273
3.	Money management	272
4.	Health education	259
5.	Attendance	254
6.	Good manners	245
7.	Take advice and instruction	242
8.	Coping with unemployment	242
9.	Time-keeping	239
10.	Family life and parenthood	237

responsibilities to bring informed judgement as democratic citizens to social issues. Their stance on the threshold of school-leaving is defensive, apprehensive and reactive (What will the world require of me?) rather than assertive and proactive (In what ways can I start to influence the world?). This may be due in part to our having focused their thoughts too exclusively upon their own immediate needs, but it

Table 4.4   Importance for Life: (b) What school-leavers under-appreciated (rank order among 27 items)

Personal Qualities:	Appearance	15th
	Work without supervision	16th
	Teamwork/co-operativeness	20th
Oral Skills:	Speak clearly	11th
	Give and seek assistance	13th
	Ask questions	17th
	Express opinions	19th
	Oral reporting	23rd
Writing Skills:	Filling in forms	14th
	Write reports	18th
Use of Graphics:	Diagrams and plans	22nd
	Maps and graphs	26th

Table 4.5   Importance for Life: (c) Some matters not mentioned by school-leavers

arms control
environmental conservation
European citizenship
gender education
global resource inequalities
human rights
information technology
inter-cultural understanding and tolerance
poverty and disadvantage

is notable that they did not accord political understanding and macro-economic awareness a high measure of importance, even though they were clear that their schools had contributed little to their understanding in these areas. In short, the requirements of responsible citizenship were much less prominent in their thoughts than those of practical citizenship.

There is evidence in the pupils' importance ratings for doubting whether schools have adequately conveyed to pupils how crucially important certain skills are. To convey accurately the various requirements of successful adulthood is no less a curriculum responsibility than that of developing what school-leavers will need to respond

Table 4.6   School-leavers' judgement of items of greatest need:
(a) for more school help   (b) for more personal preparation

Curriculum provision	(importance rating)
Money management	132
Coping with unemployment	119
Political understanding	108
Family life and parenthood	97
Health education	94
Macro-economic understanding	88
Employment and training opportunities, post-16	86
Community facilities	73
Responsibility/trustworthiness	64
Work without supervision	56

Personal preparedness	(importance rating)
Employment and training opportunities, post-16	126
Money management	106
Political understanding	73
Coping with unemployment	72
Macro-economic understanding	60
Family life and parenthood	42
Health education	20

successfully to those requirements. For example, pupils rated personal qualities overall higher than communication skills. Items involving oracy were modestly rated, nor was the widespread use of graphics (maps, graphs, diagrams and plans) fully appreciated. Furthermore, given the importance that employers attach to the abilities to work without supervision and to work co-operatively as a member of a team, one cannot be satisfied with the modest ratings pupils accorded these items. But perhaps we should not be surprised: common teaching methods emphasise neither of these abilities.

There were two particularly unexpected findings. First, pupils attached considerable importance to health education and also judged their schools to be inadequately preparing them in this area. Clearly, whatever the pupils believed they needed, they did not feel they were getting it. Unfortunately, we had not had the foresight to probe them closely on what that might be. Second, the pupils were poorly informed about courses of further education and training available to them elsewhere than in school post-16 (a finding independently confirmed by the cohort assessment programme), were well aware of their ignorance, recognised that such knowledge was important to enable them to make a wise choice, and judged their schools to have been insufficiently helpful. They wished, too, for much more guidance on how to cope with unemployment should they be faced with it. Few schools, it would appear, tackle this issue at all.

The items that were revealed as requiring the greatest degree of curriculum strengthening to match the importance pupils attach to them and remedy their sense of personal unpreparedness (see Table 4.7) are, in order of assessed current deficiency:

> money management
> knowledge of employment and training opportunities, post-16
> coping with unemployment
> political understanding
> economic understanding
> family life and parenthood
> health education

There were two main findings from the second and third interviews.

First, the young people's awareness of the importance of social skills (getting on with others, team work and capacity for co-operation), of communication skills (listening carefully, speaking clearly) and of certain personal skills related to the capacity for independent action (self-reliance, initiative) is considerably sharpened by their post-16 experiences. Second, there is evidence of considerable change of mind and plans, when what they have done is compared with the intentions they had originally expressed. Many did not get what they had sought or chose something else, and some had chosen and changed because it had not proved to be what they wanted. There is much voluntary and involuntary change of plans and much evidence of ill-considered choice.

Conclusions

The strengths of the TRAWL Project lay in its support by NICED, its association with 29 other European projects bent on similar purposes, the commitment and competence of its field officers and the enthusi-

Table 4.7   The Top Seven Needs for Curriculum Enhancement (The sum total of school-leavers discrepancy measures between ratings of importance for life and for (a) curriculum provision (b) personal preparedness.)

Money management	238
Knowledge of employment and training opportunities, post-16	212
Coping with unemployment	191
Political understanding	181
Macro-economic understanding	148
Family life and parenthood	139
Health education	114

asm of its 16 participating schools. Much was accomplished and disseminated in working papers through NICED to other schools. In particular, the project demonstrated that teachers can take corporate responsibility for determining the need for planning and implementing curriculum change and establish new modes of professional practice based on collective rather than fragmented, individualistic action. That capacity, for example, enabled the schools to recognise the value of cross-curricularity as a fertile principle of curriculum organisation.

A notable gain as a tool of curriculum evaluation has been pupil assessment and the elicitation of pupils' views of what they need to cope with the demand of adult life, their sense of preparedness to meet those demands and their views of the extent to which they have benefited from their school experiences. Another has been the recognition of the value of the out-of-school environment as a setting for promoting certain kinds of learning, and the value of out-of-school agents in contributing to this.

The work of TRAWL in the two years since the project closed has been taken forward outside of NICED by the 11–16 Curriculum Project and by the Vocational Education Project (VEP) both of which are operated jointly by the Department of Education and the Education and Library Boards. Some of the TRAWL purposes are also currently shared by the European Studies Project, which also has a link with schools in mainland Europe, and with the Secondary Science Curriculum Review. TRAWL experience has also contributed to shaping the proposed National Curriculum for Northern Ireland (DENI, 1988). Its influence is seen in the use of the concepts 'areas of study' and 'cross curricular themes' and in the importance attached to economic awareness.

There were some disappointments. Dismantling gender differences of curriculum access continues, but very slowly, and the European commitment to employing our common European heritage as an organising principle for the curriculum with a view to developing consciousness and pride in one's identity as a European has not yet gripped the imagination of the people of Northern Ireland, nor do we share a European enthusiasm for promoting political awareness in the young.

Most notably, however, TRAWL failed in the primary purpose of the EC's transition programme: 'to assist national policy formtion, 14–18'. CPVE has flourished in a few scattered areas where schools have established a co-operative relationship with their local college of further education, a development worthy of wider emulation. TVEI, 14–18, was never admitted to Northern Ireland. Educational planning remains stubbornly 5–16 and 16–19, with consequent mismatches of curriculum over the divide at 16+ and a parallel failure to provide an effective information and guidance service to young people in relation to the choices available to them for continued education and training, 16–19. Even the continuity formerly present within schools, 14–19, through GCE 'O' and 'A' level studies has been lost through the introduction of GCSE without plans to convert GCE 'A' level studies to the same educational spirit and broadened range of valued learning outcomes. The Education Reform Act confirms the government's preference for conceiving the end of compulsory schooling as an appropriate terminal point for curriculum planning.

If commitment remains to a curriculum 11–16 that addresses equally the requirements of citizenship and scholarship, there is obligation also to ensure that its range of planned learning outcomes matches appropriately all the foundation requirements of programmes on offer, 16–19. The end of compulsory schooling is no longer a natural terminal point in the process of acquiring the understanding and skills needed to respond successfully to the demands of adult and working life.

Acknowledgements are due to Mr Sean O'Kelly, formerly Chief Inspector at the Department of Education, NI, who played the major role in securing the TRAWL Project for Northern Ireland, Mr John Birch, formerly the Director of NICED, and to the TRAWL team of field officers, Mr Jack Eaton, Mrs Lorna Doherty, Ms Carmel Gallagher and Mr Cecil Holmes.

Enquiries about TRAWL are invited to Professor P.P. Daws, University of Ulster, Coleraine, Co. Londonderry, NI.

PART II

Practise What You Preach

Chapter 5

The Primary Guideline Initiative: A View from Practice

J. Billingsley
(Principal, Kines Park Primary School, Newtownabbey)

Introduction

The Primary Guideline Initiative was a rather remarkable and unique attempt at curriculum innovation throughout the primary sector. The scale and intensity of the initiative had never been attempted before in our primary schools. Various attempts at innovation had been mounted previously but they were for the most part piecemeal and limited in terms of the number of participating schools. The Primary Guideline Initiative was geared to reach into every primary school in the province. As we move forward into yet another state of change heralded by the oncoming 'National Curriculum' we could benefit greatly from a critical examination of the various aspects that have been highlighted by the experience we have gained since the Primary Guideline Initiative was launched.

It has been suggested that the 'National Curriculum' will move forward and build on the foundations of the Primary Guidelines. This claim produces a certain degree of contradiction. One of the central planks in the platform of 'Primary Guidelines' was that each school, through a process of discussion aimed at consensus and agreement should arrive at a curriculum which was best suited to the needs of the children it served. It permitted, indeed encouraged, a rich diversity of approaches which could have individual and different interpretations, even within a common geographical area. The notion of the expectations of a 'National Curriculum' does not rest comfortably with such a philosophy of individuality and diversity. Indeed, because of the overwhelming concept of uniformity that would seem to be inherent in the 'National Curriculum', one could postulate that rather than being in any way complementary, the initiatives are in fact quite the antithesis of one another.

On a more general and superficial level one could appreciate the success that the guidelines have had in engaging teachers, perhaps for the first time, in focusing on professional debate and discussion, in relation to the various components that comprise the primary curriculum. The traditional barriers of classroom isolation were broken down by such a discourse which transcended the anecdotal gossip which had for too long shackled the professional development of teachers. It still remains to be seen, however, how much discussion and debate will be encouraged by recent proposals which contain more prescription and greater uniformity. The degree of prescription related to the adherence to strict performance norms of children will be the most overt indicator of how useful the professional development was in the view of those who control and monitor our educational system.

Aims into practice

While the Primary Guideline Initiative advocated a greater level of teacher participation in curriculum development it has been claimed by some that the heightened professional awareness generated through this debate and discussion still failed to foster and secure the actual implementation of curricular innovation in the classroom situation. On close examination the lack of conceptual clarity, which permeated the initial booklet 'Introduction' (1983) it could be argued, led directly to a failure of the process at the implementation stage.

The booklet 'Introduction' (1983) suggested that principals should engage teachers in discussion aimed at producing an agreed policy statement and general philosophy for their schools. Once they had completed this task they were advised to become involved in the process of curriculum review and development in line with the general aims drawn up in the initial discussions. The model advocated in this booklet is essentially an 'aims into practice' model. This model has been present for a number of years without having the capacity to demonstrate that it possessed the necessary ingredients for the implementation of sustained and effective curriculum innovation. Indeed, when scrutinised it bears a great deal of similarity to Tyler's *Basic Principles of Curriculum and Instruction* (1948) 'rational objectives model' and derives its origins from the attempts of Bobbit (1918) and Charters (1923) to apply Taylor's (1911) principles of scientific management to education.

An 'aims into practice' model contains certain inherent dangers in terms of means-end rationality. If the means are divorced from the end a subsequent remarriage might prove well nigh impossible. Unfortunately in many cases this may have resulted in the failure to successfully implement the agreed aims. This notion of means-end rationality clearly highlights the tension that exists between the intention and reality. The initial teacher discussions about global aims represented the intention but failed to effectively penetrate the tension and reach into the actual classroom reality. Another perception of this tension can be illustrated in the relationship that exists between theory and practice.

Some of the schools that entered into the somewhat abstract debate about the general global aims of primary education found that the discussion degenerated into a search for tighter definitions and other related semantic arguments. It is perhaps understandable that this happened given the vague nature of the exercise that teachers who lacked previous experience in curriculum development would have looked for a more concrete platform. Hence the continual need for reassurance via a much more sharply focused definition. One could appreciate that this 'semantic circling' was detracting from the necessary forward movement that would have been necessary to secure implementation and bring about any real change in existing practice. Indeed, teachers have voiced more than a little disillusionment due to hours spent in discussions that seemed to go nowhere; issues that seemed to surface again and again because they had not been squarely confronted but simply redefined within a different framework.

With the publication of the first subject booklets the initial concept of the subject co-ordinator, as proposed in the Cockcroft Report (1982), was advocated and generally accepted as the best way to focus on and foster change in a particular subject area. It is interesting to note that teachers found these subject booklets very useful frameworks for examining existing practice unlike the first booklet, 'Introduction'. Unfortunately, however, with the fairly widespread appointment of co-ordinators, there arose some difficulties related to their role. The main dilemma which presented itself was whether the role was one of subject expert or simply facilitator. The notion of expert heavily outweighed that of facilitator in terms of the general perceptions of teachers. Once teachers were identified as co-ordinators other teachers saw the writing and production of the particular guideline as almost the sole responsibility of those teachers. This unintended but evolved outcome undermined the whole philopsophy of the 'guidelines' of consensus and agreement. The criticism of the Inspectorate Survey (1981) that:

It is disturbing that so many schools have no general guidelines for

the teachers; and that even when they are available, so many teachers have an inadequate appreciation of them . . ..
The survey shows that even when they are available the curriculum
guidelines prepared by Principals for their staff, tend to lack clarity
and direction.   (DENI, pp. 8 and 9)

Certainly, teacher appreciation of guidelines would not be enhanced
by the delegation to one person of the responsibility for their production and development. Indeed, it could be argued with some
justification that in the cases where the role has been perceived as one
of expert, we have turned full circle from where the principal drew up
guidelines to where this responsibility has been simply delegated to a
single teacher. The awarding of promoted posts to subject co-
ordinators could also be seen to cause a certain teacher alienation in
that other teachers could opt out feeling that the co-ordinator was
receiving a monetary reward and therefore should assume total responsibility. One of the main strengths of the guideline initiative was the
notion of shared responsibility through attempts to reach consensus as
to what should comprise the primary curriculum, this strength could
be seriously undermined if the co-ordinator role is one of expert. The
concept of facilitator does not possess any of these detrimental qualities
however and if clearly defined will foster staff involvement or 'ownership' which curriculum developers feel to be absolutely essential for
successful implementation.

Accountability in primary education

Accountability in education has mushroomed at an alarming rate from
the heady days of the 1977 Green Paper, Callaghan's Ruskin Speech,
the Great Debate and now into the 'National Curriculum'. It is worth
reflecting upon the consequences of heightened accountability which
were emerging during the Primary Guideline Initiative. It should be
remembered that the need for curricular guidelines was raised by the
Department of Education's Inspectorate in the Primary Survey (1981)
and while they refused to be prescriptive they passed the initiative to
the Northern Ireland Council for Educational Development. However,
although NICED claimed independence, it had been established at the
behest of the Department of Education and the Department of Education's Inspectorate had a high profile in terms of representation at
both central and working party levels. To some teachers it seemed that

those who had first raised the questions about guidelines were also answering the questions from within the structures of NICED.

In the climate of spiralling accountability, contractual accountability was to loom large in the perception of teachers. Out of contractual accountability grew the need for some schools to react in terms of superficial compliance – they felt they had to move in certain directions. The main danger was that they were simply complying with what they thought the educational establishment wanted or indeed required and not from a position of an acknowledged commitment to change. Teacher commitment is acclaimed as being an essential ingredient of successful curriculum development – the very spine of any educational enterprise and yet it was an aspect that seemed to receive scant attention from those in control of the initiative. When teachers move from a traditionally held position without being fully convinced of the need for change, they sometimes find themselves in a somewhat neutral position which lacks the justification of previous commitment. Some would argue that the pressure of mounting contractual accountability being applied centrally from the Department of Education and locally from Education and Library Boards could have combined to produce this undesirable aspect of superficial compliance. Certainly it would be accepted that innovation can be encouraged but successful educational innovation cannot be forced.

Another far-reaching aspect of accountability in the model advocated by NICED was in relation to the formulation of general aims. If a school has the ability to formulate general aims which are consistent with classroom practice, it will enhance professional autonomy since it may be well able to determine where aspects of accountability reside. If, however, the exercise of formulating aims is divorced from classroom practice earlier referred to with reference to means-end rationality a mismatch between what the school says it is doing and what it actually is doing will have been created. The emergence of such a state of mismatch will have serious ramifications for any school especially in terms of contractual accountability. If such a state is present then contractual accountability will have been substantially increased with a reciprocal diminution in professional autonomy. Crucial to any examination of this area of accountability is the fact that the 'aims and objectives' movement was not introduced or intended as an aid to the classroom teacher but as a method of establishing a framework of structure from which to evaluate educational outcomes.

Practice into aims

When teachers use aims and objectives they create frameworks from which their own performance can be monitored and evaluated. If a dichotomy exists between the intention of the aim and the reality of existing school practice it will have exposed quite unwittingly a vulnerability to those who evaluate the system. It should be remembered also that this was all taking place in a climate of a changing and much more intensive and probing General Inspection format, arrived at by the Department of Education's Inspectorate; outcomes of which were being published in the local press.

Teachers experienced difficulty in formulating aims either in looking for the insurance of an all encompassing statement or by defining aims so tightly that they rendered themselves very limited and almost meaningless. The Schools Council, 'Aims of Primary Education Project' attempted to explain why teachers experience difficulty in the formulation of aims:

> At least part of the difficulty may stem from the fact that on the whole, teachers are neither required nor encouraged to formulate their aims. But more than that, aims are tightly related to practice and the need to cope with demands of teaching tends to shift the focus on to practice rather than on to aims.   (1975, p. 3)

So previously teachers had not been involved in discussions about general aims and indeed would clearly identify their major area of concern as practice. If this promise is accepted then it follows that any initiative, if it is to succeed, must be firmly based on existing practice. Schools Council Working Paper *Primary Practice* clearly identified an alternative model, namely 'Practice to Aims' and described it as follows:

> Another approach is to start from what the School is already doing and try to decide what aims are implied by current practice . . ..
> This practice to aims approach ensures that the exercise is rooted in the realities of school life, and is moreover a necessary part of the critical evaluation that must take place before any change is made.   (1975 p. 119)

Since teachers have had relatively limited experience in the formulation of aims it was seen by some as a retrograde step to plunge teachers into the abstract amorphousness inherent in discussions about the global aims of primary education. The almost total concentration on aims produced a studied ignorance of the existing practice which had evolved over a period of time.

Those who criticised the aims into practice approach advocated by the booklet 'Introduction' cited that it would be far more effective to carry out an indepth review and examination of existing curricular practice in order to extract the implicit aims of that practice. Once this had been achieved an explicit statement of curricular aims could be made. Once these aims had been made explicit it was felt, by those who advocated this approach, that they could be critically scrutinised to ensure that they were both desirable and comprehensive. If they were found wanting in this regard they could be changed with comparative ease. Undertaking such a review with each curricular area being considered independently would ensure that aims and practice remained synchronised and that necessary change would be affected as a gradual and evolutionary process. A central purpose in choosing this 'way forward' was to avoid the danger of a rift between general aims and practice for which NICED's chosen model had much potential. Supporting this notion was the incremental process of focusing on one area of the curriculum at a time which would also be a valuable staff development exercise culminating in the ultimately acquired teacher confidence and competence necessary to deal finally with the much more difficult task of formulating the general aims of the school.

It is interesting to note that the failure of the 'Introductory Booklet' to identify any other approaches led to a widespread debate which was ultimately to force NICED into acknowledging that schools could choose an approach other than the failed 'aims into practice'. It was unfortunate that NICED's booklet 'Introduction' had gone more than a little way in confusing the whole issue of school review. Its initial failure to take account of other models was viewed by some as a form of prescription by omission.

Resource provision

Another aspect of the Guideline Initiative which deserves some examination was in the field of resource provision. An extremely tight central control was exercised over the allocation of resources. When viewed in the context of the 11–16 Programme, its counterpart in the secondary sphere, the Primary Guidelines seemed to be an extremely impoverished relation. It lacked the autonomy over financial delegation that was evident in the 11–16 Programme. Indeed, because of its tight central control it would be seen as being resource driven rather than needs driven. Those sitting at the centre of the network decided what the school should receive rather than delegating the necessary finance so that schools could ascertain their own needs and meet them as they arose. Another factor that quickly became evident was that the structures of financing and resourcing primary education were so rigid that all too often imaginative strategies, for meeting the needs of those schools involved in innovation, were trapped within their own confining structures.

Conclusion

The dissemination process of the guidelines was an example of how, when the central control of those initiating an innovatory exercise relaxed their control, delegation became somewhat disjointed. The Education and Library Boards which had been given responsibility for the dissemination process set about devising strategies which would best permeate the schools they served. Unfortunately the strategies deployed varied greatly from one Board to another and this led to more than a little confusion as to which was the best way to proceed to successfully effect curriculum implementation. Some Boards seem to be more generous in their interpretation of how resources could be used and this caused schools to make comparisons between Board areas.

There are few genuine innovatory attempts that are flawless – certainly the Primary Guideline Initiative had its flaws, some of a fairly fundamental nature which caused more than a little confusion on the educational scene in Northern Ireland. The volume and intensity of initiated changes left teachers stunned and reeling. The sheer proliferation of educational initiatives largely undermined the professional confidence of serving teachers. The resulting confusion has meant that teachers are almost looking forward to the 'National Curriculum' feeling a need for an operational platform which appears to teachers, at any rate, to have a much more concrete composition. It is rather ironic that the failure of the Primary Guideline Initiative should spawn an atmosphere which would be conducive to 'the way forward'.

Chapter 6

The Development of an Integrated School

Peter McGaffin
(Principal, Hazelwood Integrated Primary School, Newtownabbey)

'The trouble about us here in Ulster', said Lord Glentoran ' . . . is that we get excited about education and drink.' (Akenson, *Education and Enmity*, 1973). A lesser mortal might have added that probably it is education which drives us to drink, but perhaps that is placing a conclusion where one might reasonably expect an introduction, so let me suggest what the reader can expect in this chapter.

I do not propose to discuss the Northern Ireland educational scene in general, for that lies elsewhere in this book, but I will highlight those aspects which have contributed directly to the present integrated system. Nor is it my intention to discuss those invaluable programmes and organisations which aim to help the children and schools of the controlled and Catholic-maintained sectors to understand each other more readily.

What I hope to do is show the reader what it has been like opening and developing an integrated school, in one particular area of Belfast. I do not presume the ability or the right to speak for any other teacher in any other integrated school, nor for the integrated movement in general. Rather, what follows is a subjective history of one school, 1985–89.

In the beginning

The reader should be aware that integrated schooling is not a new development in Belfast. As early as 1812, Nicholas Grimshaw built a large two-storey building near Greencastle. It was a mixed school, with both boys and girls, Protestants and Catholics. Religious education was taught daily, with extra time on Thursdays. About 1877 the Roman Catholic authorities opened a new school near the railway station at Greencastle. It was made quite clear to those Protestants concerned that they were most welcome, and many did in fact continue their education there, but in 1892 Whitehouse Presbyterian opened its own new

school near Mount Street. Eventually Greencastle School became a
national school, and some of the children were moved from one school
to another when parents were dissatisfied with progress or with a certain teacher (Armstrong, 1979). (The reader should note the fact that
parents often chose schools on the basis of teaching standards rather
than the presence or absence of their co-religionists, for this is a point
to which I will return.)

Attempts were also made by the state to establish a non-denominational system of schools in 1831 and again, just after partition in 1920.

> The fact remains, however, that the most important theme
> running through Northern Ireland's educational history has been
> the seemingly irresistible demand for segregated schooling . . . .
> Despite their detestation of each other, the educational principles
> of Protestant and Catholic clergymen have been remarkably
> similar on pivotal issues.   (Akenson, 1977)

This attitude seems to have continued to the modern day.

The early eighties

In 1979 Throne Primary School in north Belfast faced potential closure
due to the declining birth rate and shifts in population. The management committee of the school felt that integration would be one way of
boosting enrolment and so maintaining the school's service to the local
community.

However, although the Belfast Education and Library Board (BELB)
supported, and the Department of Education (DENI) granted, this
application for a change of status, in making its nominations for the
management committee of the new Throne Integrated Primary School
the BELB chose to nominate managers who were drawn exclusively
from the non-Catholic sector. While such nominations may well have
been made on the basis of merit, there can be little doubt that in the
political climate of the early 1980s they served to create the impression
that the granting of integrated status was little more than a facade. Such
impressions were reinforced by the fact that, not only was the management committee exclusively non-Catholic, but so too was the teaching
and ancillary staff. The school principal asked the BELB to appoint a
further teacher (who would be Catholic), but the Board chose not to
exercise that power. Further, the Catholic Church chose not to exercise
its right to nominate representatives.

Thus, from the very beginning, Throne Integrated Primary School was integrated in name only. The result was that while a number of Catholic families showed interest in the enterprise, extremely few of them took their interest beyond the first step of making enquiries. Enrolment continued to decline until, in August 1985, with only 28 children on the rolls, the school closed permanently.

A few years earlier, with the support of All Children Together (ACT), a group of parents had opened the first planned integrated school. On 1 September 1981, Lagan College opened to the south of the city, with 28 secondary-age children. Despite the success of Lagan College, in the years between 1981 and 1985 no other integrated school opened, the reasons being threefold.

In the first place, and perhaps most importantly, many of those directly involved with Lagan College were only too aware of the extremely precarious financial position of the school, having to rely entirely on charitable donations, fund-raising and parental contributions. It was realised that if other integrated schools were to open, they would be making financial calls on the same limited pot and, by doing so, might well jeopardise the very existence of Lagan College.

In the second place, the powers that be and society in general seemed to look on Lagan College as an interesting one-off that could be tolerated. For example, speaking of integrated education in 1982, Cardinal Tomas O'Fiaich said:

> . . . the only place I can see for it at the moment is for experiments like Lagan College in Belfast, and in striving for a closer inter-relationship between the two school systems in the North . . .'.
>
> (O'Fiaich, 1982)

The fact that Lagan College was fee-paying (albeit with the availability of numerous bursaries) led many, without ever producing any evidence, to view the school as being for 'the well-off middle class who fail the Eleven Plus'. This view was even put forward a few years before Lagan College opened, with Akenson concluding that:

> . . . to be successful an integrated institution should be constituted on children of parents who have . . . shared beliefs about communal harmony being more important than religious purity . . . this implies, unfortunately, that for the foreseeable future the successfully integrated schools probably will be class-bound institutions.
>
> (Akenson, 1977)

The third reason for the failure to open other integrated schools lay within the philosophy of ACT. In the main, ACT saw its role as one of supporting those groups which might ask for help. and therefore did not actively encourage such groups to come forward. Therein lay the seeds of discontent. In the same year that Lagan College achieved grant-aided status (1984), and in the midst of Throne Primary School's struggle to survive as an integrated school, one of the Officers of ACT produced a Five Year Plan which essentially aimed at expanding integrated education, not only into other secondary schools similar to Lagan College, but also into the primary sector. After lengthy discussion ACT decided against adopting the plan. It was felt strongly that Lagan College needed further help and assistance, but in particular there was a reaction against the proposed change in attitude, the plan having implied that ACT should actively seek out interested groups who would then be sheltered, supported and perhaps fortified.

The result was that a number of those involved in ACT decided to promote the Five Year Plan outside the auspices of ACT, and in October 1984 the Belfast Charitable Trust for Integrated Education (BELTIE) was established.

Establishing the school

Among BELTIE's aims were:

a) The implementation of the Five Year Plan previously presented to ACT; and

b) the creation of the model which Local Education and Library Boards might follow in the promotion of integrated education,

seeing its role as one of actively identifying and encouraging the 'need' for integrated education rather than simply responding to an expressed need.

A number of the parents of Throne Integrated Primary School (due to close in August 1985) were contacted and invited to play an active role in small groups which would meet regularly in the north Belfast area with the aim of examining the viability of establishing an integrated school in the area.

At this point I would ask the reader to pause, and to consider briefly the role of parents in Northern Irish schools.

During the 1945–50 period Bishop Farren of Derry claimed that the government's reason for having civic and parental representatives on a school management committee was a hollow one because the Catholic clerical school manager was not just an individual but the holder of a religious office, and as such was automatically taken by the Catholic people as their representative (Akenson, 1977). While the Bishop openly articulated the Catholic position on lay representation, it should be borne in mind that the main difference between the Catholic Church and its Protestant counterparts has been that no individual has been able to speak with the same authority for all Protestants. The fact remains, however, that the attitude of the Protestant clergy was little different from that expressed by the Bishop. The result was that until the late 1970s the involvement of parents in Ulster schools was limited to a minority of schools. For most schools, parental involvement was honoured more in the breach than the observance, and was often little more than a cosmetic exercise.

Given this lack of parental experience in running schools it was hardly surprising that those parents invited to meet with representatives of BELTIE were both enthusiastic and receptive. What was surprising was the poor standard of advice that they were given. Considering that BELTIE itself only came into existence in October 1984, it is little short of amazing that by February 1985 the parents had been persuaded of the viability of opening not one, but TWO integrated schools in north Belfast – a primary school (with nursery) and a secondary college – both to open in September 1985.

The reader might well ask whether or not anyone considered the potential cost of the proposed schools, and the answer is that indeed they did. At a public meeting held in April 1985, a direct question from a potential parent specifically asked how the schools would be funded. The answer, from a representative of BELTIE, was that the schools would be non-fee paying; that BELTIE was committed to their success, and would provide adequate funding to ensure the establishment of the schools, and their survival, until they achieved grant-aided status. Unfortunately, no one present at the meeting thought it necessary to ask whether or not BELTIE had the wherewithal to meet that commitment. The answer only became clear over the following year with the primary school (of which I became principal) only surviving by dint of running up very large debts and an even larger overdraft.

However, if we might remain with the parental working parties and the advice they were given in early 1985, one might ask what the aims of the school were to be. One would be tempted to suggest 'integration', but in fact a press release of February 1985 stated:

The overriding philosophy of the schools will be the equal

> responsibility of the home and the school for the education of the
> children.   (BELTIE, 1985)

That might have been well-and-good, considering the comments
made above regarding parental involvement, but a leaflet distributed at
the public meeting in April stated:

> The overriding aim of the schools will be the promotion of child-
> centred education.   (BELTIE, 1985)

It did not seem to occur to anyone to ask just what these statements
meant, much less suggest that there might be a conflict. I am tempted
to recall the comment of Sir Kenneth Cork in his autobiography *Cork on
Cork* when, dealing with the De Lorean saga, he wrote:

> Colourful characters who lack self-discipline need strong-minded
> colleagues to keep them in balance, particularly when they have
> made themselves dependent on other people's money.
>
> (Cork, 1985)

The events of 1984–85 were, I think, a case of strong-minded and
persuasive characters convincing the parents, via jargon and high-flown
waffle, that theirs would be a fine school and that anything was possible,
without having the courage or self-discipline to detail for those parents
the sheer hard work and the degree of finance that would be required
in order to achieve even minimal progress.

Apart from the funding of the school, most of the questions posed at
the public meeting centred upon:

a) Religious Education; and
b) the curriculum and how it would be developed.

Those who raised the issue of Religious Education appeared, in the
main, to be concerned with two problems:

a) relationships with, and/or the attitude of, the Catholic Church; and
b) whether or not children of different faiths would be taught together
   or separately.

They were assured that firm contacts had been established with
the Catholic Church, and that there would be no problems over the
confirmation of P7 children, nor for 7 year-olds receiving their First
Communion. They were also told that members of the Catholic clergy
were willing to come into the school. They were also referred to the
leaflet which had been distributed and which stated:

> Extra support will be provided to both teachers and parents through seminars and courses . . . .   (BELTIE, 1985)

At the numerous meetings of parents and of governors which took place from May through August 1985, it became apparent to both myself and the chairperson of the School Board that there existed a great deal of vagueness and ambiguity regarding the term 'integration'. When we raised the matter, the Development Officer of BELTIE arranged a seminar to discuss the issue. At the seminar, one of the BELTIE officers outlined the requirements of a 'planned' integrated school.

Those present at the seminar accepted that the religious balance within the school should never be outside a 60:40 Protestant:Catholic ratio, and that this should apply to both children, staff and governors. These, and other points, have been detailed by Mr Tony Spencer. He argued, then and since, that:

> having both Principal and Vice-Principal from the same community would seriously weaken confidence in the school's integrated character.   (Spencer, 1985)

He further argued that integrated schools must offer the Irish language, Gaelic games, Irish dancing and music, as options to all pupils. He did not say, but one presumes that these options should be in addition to various non-Gaelic games, non-Irish dancing and music. Significantly he did not say where the finance, expertise, resources and facilities for such a range of activities were to come from.

1985–88

And so the school opened in September 1985.

Suddenly, I and five other teachers faced the problem of implementing, in the classroom, the various aims and philosophies that were, quite honestly, as clear as mud. To some extent the problems did not arise right away. We had 99 children on the rolls, covering the full nursery and primary age-range of 3–11. Over 50 of the children were 6+ and had transferred from other primary schools. Simply helping the children to settle in, and dealing with the everyday problems that all teachers face, took up enough of our time, but it gradually dawned on me that many of the assurances we had been given, particularly those regarding religion and finance, were little more than hot air.

Religious education

The one inescapable fact of Northern Ireland's educational development has been that the raising of the subject of religious education has
always initiated bitter religious controversy. As a Member of Parliament
noted during the marathon four-day debate on the White Paper on
educational reconstruction during the period 1945–50, 'it is perfectly
obvious that ninety-five percent of the debate on the educational proposals in this house, outside it, and in the press, has ranged round the
religious instruction question . . . '. That MP might well have been
describing the meetings that took place in the school throughout the
year 1985–86, for religious education took up so much time that no
other curricular matter was discussed, despite the protestations of the
school staff and a number of parents. Indeed, because of the hours
spent discussing the same religious issues a substantial number of
parents (of both persuasions) expressed a determination to never again
attend parents' meetings in the school.

Considering that the problem has been some centuries in the
making, it would be presumptuous of me to claim any sort of solution,
but suffice it to say that for the time being we had reached a com-
promise, albeit an unsatisfactory one, which worked.

In the first place, with the invaluable assistance of the Peace Education Officer of the Irish Council of Churches, I arranged a series of
seven seminars and a residential weekend at which staff and parents
could discuss the issue, and by the spring of 1986 I felt we had reached
agreement on how and what to teach in religious education, an agreement that was acceptable to the teachers and to the majority of parents.
Within weeks, however, a very small number of Catholic parents
demanded (which is not too strong a word) that the children be
separated for religious education, citing the assurance given by BELTIE
that religious education would be provided 'according to the wishes of
parents'. Despite the fact that there were only a few families involved,
they brought so much pressure to bear on the School Board that it was
agreed to separate the children for one session of denominational
instruction each week.

During the same period approaches were made to the Catholic
Church, to discuss the matter further. It became clear that while the
Church would not oppose integrated education, neither would it offer
any support. It adhered to the view that simple Bible teaching
was based on the fundamental principle of Protestantism, and
was unacceptable to Roman Catholics. In Osborne *et al* (1988),
G. Loughran has pointed out that:

> For Catholic education ... religious education cannot be compartmentalised or limited to a specific timetable period in the school day.
>
> (Loughran, 1988)

Consequently, in order to meet more readily the requirements of the Catholic Church, the position at present is that for two sessions each week the children and teachers split along denominational lines, with classes for Sacramental preparation being provided in addition to three other sessions of general religious education.

It should not be thought that this situation is satisfactory to any of the participating groups, there being, for example, a number of Catholic parents who oppose the denominational split required by their co-religionists. It is, however, acceptable for the time being. What the future brings remains to be seen, but there is little doubt in my mind that much of the aggravation was caused in 1985 by certain individuals making claims and giving assurances for which they had no justification whatsoever.

Finance and resources

Earlier in the chapter I raised the matter of the poor advice, and indeed the lack of advice, given to the original parents. In terms of finance and resources this had a number of implications. To the teaching staff, the immediate problem was a lack of resources.

From the very first day, and running like a bad dream through the following three years, the school lacked resources. Not, I might add, in the manner that all schools and all teachers complain of lacking resources, but fundamentally and most seriously lacking, to the extent that we began to feel that the Israelite slaves of Ancient Egypt had been well-off in only having to collect their own straw. (At least they had mud!) For the new school, a substantial amount of secondhand and outdated books and equipment had been acquired by teachers begging from colleagues in other schools. There was not a single area of the curriculum which was adequately, much less properly, resourced, to the extent that individual teachers bought and provided some of the resources needed by their particular classes. (The teacher of the P6–7 children, for example, personally provided the reading materials for the 13 children in the class.)

The then treasurer and Board of the school might well feel aggrieved at these comments, considering that they provided some £3000–£4000 to equip the school. They failed to appreciate, however, that at that time other schools were receiving some £3000 as an annual topping-up allowance. Having to completely furnish and equip a school on such a budget was impossible. This issue led to other, related, problems.

It became clear to the staff that the financial standing of the school was, to be diplomatic, very delicately poised. On a number of occasions the teachers were genuinely unsure as to whether or not they would be paid at the end of the month. I did my best as principal to reassure them and so keep their minds on the educational problems, but knowing even more than they did about the precarious financial position, and needing my salary every bit as much as they did, I know that my reassurances rang hollow. Consequently, we all worked under the shadow of continuous financial threat, with the closure of the school and our subsequent redundancy a very real possibility. Personally, I felt a great deal of stress in trying to reassure teachers at a time when I was under even greater pressure than they were for precisely the same reasons, and only feeling grateful that they were not aware of the whole truth.

The pressure that this created was compounded when, in 1986, we learnt that due to bureaucratic bungling in some quarters of the school Board, our superannuation payments had never been made to DENI. Consequently I and several other teachers faced a break-in-service that could have serious repercussions on our pensionable rights, a problem that persists to this day.

The second problem related to the poor financing of the school, and following on from the pressures that the teachers felt themselves to be under, was parent-teacher relationships.

A number of parents, and it must be said that it was a small minority of parents, seemed continually to make critical comments about what teachers were doing, or not doing. This is probably a feature of every single school in the British Isles, but considering the pressures that the teachers of this school were already under, and the fact that on a number of occasions they personally paid for resources, it led teachers to feel that parents did nothing but complain.

I must repeat that in practice this was limited to a small number of parents and Board members. The vast majority of parents were very complimentary and supportive, but it seems to be part of human nature for comliments to be forgotten while criticisms cut deeply. Teachers suffer from such foibles as much as anyone else, with the result that to an even greater extent the teachers felt under pressure and, further, that theirs was an utterly thankless task.

It should be pointed out, of course, that the survival and viability of the school was every bit as important to the parents as to the teachers.

It was noted earlier that even in the 19th century parents tended to pick and choose schools on the basis of standards of education and that rightly remains the case today. Despite some of the woolly-headed would-be prophets that the school continues to suffer from, most parents remain quite clear-headed about what they want for their children. It would be a most unusual parent who would sacrifice their child's education on the altar of integration, with the result that over the past three years 99% of parents who made enquiries about enrolling their child sought reassurance on the long-term viability of the school and its standards. Until the school achieved grant-aid from DENI it would have been professional suicide, for both me and for the school, to have openly admitted to prospective parents the poor resourcing and general financial position of the school. For both personal and professional reasons I could not lie to parents, but sought instead to reassure them by pointing to the herculean efforts of the staff and of the school Board, and by referring them to the satisfaction already expressed by many parents. Nonetheless, it created a great deal of pressure and stress for me to have to reassure parents when I was still seeking answers to the very questions that they were asking.

The children

In retrospect, one of the mistakes that we made was to accept children of too wide an age-range. Originally intended to involve infant ages only, the school opened with eight age groups, Nursery to Primary 7. That in itself was not a problem, there only being some 15–20 children in each class, but undoubtedly a number of parents transferred to the school children who had social, academic and/or behavioural problems in other schools, in the hope or expectation that a new school with smaller classes would solve the problems. Inevitably the children in question were enrolled before we discovered the potential problems, so there was little we could do other than somehow deal with the matter. The consequences have been twofold.

In the first place the behaviour of those children, even though a minority, set a poor example that younger children copied, to the general detriment of the school. Even though most of those children have now left the school a pattern has been created that will take some years to reform. Behaviour, therefore, while never beyond control, got off to a rather poor start, and has taken up a great deal more of the teachers' time and effort than was expected.

The second, closely related aspect, was that in its first two years the school enrolled more than its fair share of low-achievers. In itself this is not a problem. Indeed, thanks to the professionalism of the teachers the school has gained a reputation for successfully tackling problems which have been beyond the capabilities of some other schools. In the present educational climate, however, with schools being judged on 'results' the school appears to perform poorly relative to some others in the area.

There is no short-term answer to either of these problems. Provided the teachers continue to perform as they have done for the past three years, I have no doubt that their reputations and that of the school can only be enhanced. Until then, the school still needs to sell itself, and to prove itself, on educational grounds.

Growing pains

In this, its fourth year, the school has 225 children enrolled. In August 1985 there were some 70 children on the rolls with a planned staff of 4 teachers. By the start of the school year there were 99 pupils. Once parents saw the school as a living entity, others put their children forward, so that by the end of the first year there were nearly 120 pupils and 6 staff. Naturally this created budgetary problems, but in the main highlighted a communication problem.

When I proposed to the Board that extra staff be employed in the autumn of 1985, it was discussed at length and duly agreed. Some months later, the Chairperson of BELTIE commented that the first she had known of the matter was when she had seen the relevant advertisements in the press. Further, she and the BELTIE Treasurer intimated that many of the financial problems were a result of the school employing staff without consulting BELTIE (which was responsible for meeting the bills) and that as a result BELTIE faced budgetary problems. The fact that BELTIE had two representatives on the school Board was conveniently ignored, as was the fact that the Development Officer of BELTIE had fully participated in the relevant Board decisions.

A 225% increase in pupil numbers since 1985 speaks volumes for the success of the school, but think for one moment of some 200 children trying to play in a playground suitable for perhaps 50; of P1's working in rooms suitable in space for far older children; of infants soiling themselves because their rooms are upstairs and the nearest toilets are downstairs; of having to turn away potential pupils or else to have 30+ children in rooms which were crowded with 25.

Think too of a building which is vandalised every few weeks, and burgled regularly; of a roof which leaks in more places than one cares to think about; of ceilings which have collapsed in two places.

Consider too the fact that the school now caters for a catchment area served by some 30–40 'normal' schools, and the subsequent problems and cost involved in transporting those young children to and from school each day.

I am the first to admit that such problems are all too common in far too many schools, for I have worked in some of them and visited numerous others, but I doubt if many other schools suffer ALL of these problems to the same degree. Other schools, too, do not have to prove themselves in the same manner as does a new integrated school.

Conclusion

The integrated school is not designed to replace either of the existing school systems, nor to compete with them. The integrated school is simply offered to parents as an alternative.

Those parents are drawn from all social backgrounds. In contradiction of Akenson's conclusion that 'the successfully integrated schools probably will be class-bound institutions', and in spite of the claims of certain narrow-minded local politicians, the school is most definitely not limited to the well-off middle class, but rather covers a wider social spectrum than almost any other primary school of comparable size.

But would I do it all over again? No! Not if I had to face the same problems again, but others will, I hope, have learned from our experience. Lest it is not yet clear and you are thinking of opening such a school, let me summarise.

1. If those planning the school have been doing so for less than a year, look for another job.
   I feel that perhaps half of the problems we faced had their genesis in the fact that the entire planning process took only eleven months. For lack of time far too much was generalised, neglected and, at times, simply ignored.
2. When you are assured that such-and-such a matter has been dealt

with, demand explicit and written confirmation of it. In particular, beware of such assurances when they are given by colourful, persuasive and strong-minded characters who do not enrol their own children in such a school. If those assurances are not explicit, and in writing, look for another job.

3. Insist on seeing a detailed budget for the school covering, at minimum, the approaching school year. If and when anyone proposes enrolling children or employing staff which will lead to the budget being exceeded, refuse to permit it. Or look for another job.

4. Insist that the proposed premises be surveyed by a qualified and independent surveyor, and insist upon seeing and discussing the surveyor's report. Then go back to the budget and ensure that it covers the cost of repairs as detailed by the surveyor!

5. Before the school opens, insist that the aims, philosophy and ethos of the school are fully discussed and agreed. Be especially careful that their attainment is within the bounds of reason. One of the major problems was that comments made by some of those not directly responsible for the school led to an unreasonable level of expectations among the parent body. The staff of the school often felt the need to define their actions rather than, as they have been entitled to do, trumpet their own achievements.

6. When anyone suggests what an integrated school could or should do in order to prove itself truly integrated, go back to step No. 2 and start again. In particular, demand evidence that that person is able and willing to provide the facilities and finance needed to do what he or she proposes for the school.

7. Insist upon a job description. Without one, it is too easy for everything that others neglect to be left at your doorstep and, if you then fail to deal with it, you will be held responsible. Equally, you should require that the responsibilities and remit of the various committees and groups involved in the school be spelt out in some detail.

8. For the curricular policies of such a new school, err on the side of being too prescriptive. Teachers have their weaknesses as much as any other profession and one cannot afford mistakes in the early stages.

9. Think seriously of working in another school.

Chapter 7

Notes on Working with Less Able Boys in West Belfast

Gerry Ruddy
(Teacher, Corpus Christi College, Belfast)

Introduction

This chapter gives an account of my introduction to teaching less able boys. It concentrates on the attitudes and values of teachers who work in difficult circumstances in west Belfast. By examining a number of case studies of less able pupils, and sharing my experience of working with difficult boys with colleagues this chapter will highlight the social and economic problems found in west Belfast.

Teaching in the Whiterock

In the middle of 1972 I began teaching in west Belfast. It was a time of civil unrest and of large-scale population shifts. When I worked in St Thomas' Secondary School in the Whiterock, Ballymurphy area of west Belfast the headmaster was a man of boundless energy, immense sympathy and rather traditional views on education. He had a huge task on his hands for the turmoil outside could not but affect life inside the school. Two of our school chaplains were shot dead, many of our pupils had fathers either gaoled, interned, wounded or killed in the conflict. Indeed some of the pupils would go on to meet the same fate.

Despite the 'troubles' and the poverty of the area, the school had a commendable record in producing 'achievement'. A number of my teaching colleagues had gone to the school as pupils, and were more than happy to return as teachers. They felt an affinity with the school and there was certainly a strong bond that existed between teachers and pupils. Meeting ex-pupils many years later, I was always struck by their obvious affection for both the school and some of the teachers. Many of the less able pupils were positive in their attitudes to the school. They felt the school had tried to help them and they perceived the benefits of schooling even if they themselves had not always gained from the experience.

Culture shock

Before coming to west Belfast I had already had some teaching experience having taught in St Joseph's Intermediate in Newry. I had undertaken a one year post-graduate course in St Joseph's College, where I had specialised in history and social education. Unfortunately some of the lecturers had no experience of what it was like to teach in a secondary school, their own experiences being totally grammar school orientated. So long as grammar schools are in existence, secondary schools and subsequently their pupils, will be seen as second rate even by those who 'own' the schools. Some people see the pupils only through the light of their own grammar school education. Indeed, I initially had the same problem. I didn't know of the existence of less able pupils. Their world was not mine. And yet here I was, a CBS grammar school and university educated pupil ready to 'help' these unfortunates.

I learned quickly that sympathy for the 'underdog' was insufficient to achieve concrete results with less able pupils. As is the case with most other teachers I learned on the job. In my day-to-day contact with the pupils I began to recognise my own inadequacies and my own mistakes. Years of teaching the less able has convinced me that I have still an enormous amount to learn about creating the necessary conditions for the young people to learn in.

Meeting the less able

My introduction to the less able in west Belfast was a 3F class in St Thomas'. I had this class for history, and it was quite a shock. The classroom itself was at that time used by a number of different classes. Consequently desks were untidy, rubbish from the bin regularly thrown about the floor and windows often smashed. The class was the lowest stream in the school. One of the pupils in 3F was 'Eugene' a dark-skinned boy with rather narrow eyes which led to an unfortunate nickname. His home circumstances were very poor, one parent absent, the other an alcoholic. He regularly came to school dirty and smelling to high heaven. His conversation, such as it was, was difficult to understand because of a speech impediment. His pencils were usually tiny stubs held in his dirty hands. Eugene had no social skills whatsoever. In school he was always in trouble with teachers and in the days of corporal punishment was regularly in the wars. Along with 'Joseph' a close friend, Eugene would rarely sit still, was always acting the lig and generally infuriating every adult that came in contact with him. Yet, in spite of all the mischief, both pupils were liked by those teachers who took time to get to know them. They responded to such teachers by being slightly less disruptive in their classes.

The school established a bank of what I considered empathic teachers. An empathic teacher was one who had a commitment to teaching less able pupils, could see their point of view, wanted to work with them and was prepared to act as a 'base' teacher for a class. Usually during the third term I would informally approach teachers, seeking out those who seemed to have the right attitudes and sounding them out to see if they would become a 'base' teacher for the coming school year. Having established my bank of teachers and ascertained both the classes and rooms available I would then submit a provisional timetable to senior management. Invariably the finished timetable would be very different from our proposals but I usually managed to retain some element of what I wanted.

Each class should have a 'base' teacher who took that class for at least two subjects out of English, maths, geography, religious education and life skills. The class had responsibility for their classroom which they had to decorate with their work and keep clean. (This was not always successful.) The theory behind the 'base' classroom and teacher was that it cut down movement and personnel, enabling stability and familiarity to develop. Consequently, because for the most part they were with teachers who were all the time trying to develop empathy with them, the pupils were less likely to cause trouble and, therefore, more likely to work. In relative terms I believe I was successful. Teachers of the more academic streams on the occasions of their contact with less able pupils, would compliment the less able classes on their behaviour.

Discipline

Once when called to the telephone, I left eighteen fourth years alone in the class with work to do and the door open. In my absence the head-master came in, walked around and went out, noticed only by a few of the pupils who lifted their head from their work. He later complimented the class on their behaviour. That discipline of the class was a self-discipline. Their work was interesting; they were motivated so they needed little external discipline.

Classes were named after their teacher so for a number of years healthy competition developed between 5H and 5R. 5H indeed managed to get their own exclusive football kit which they wore proudly against other schools. The role of the teacher was crucial to this. He had to identify with the class, check up on absenteeism, meet parents and sort out discipline problems with other teachers. This is not to say 'base' teachers didn't have discipline problems. Indeed, we all did. But because of our close proximity to one another we could refer a pupil to a colleague quickly in situations which might possibly lead to violence. This usually worked by enabling all sides to calm down and allowed the teachers to resolve the difficulties and return to the conditions where self-discipline could be exercised.

Over the period of one or two years the 'base' teacher and class would get to know each other. The class would know what behaviour was acceptable. Whenever they misbehaved the teacher's general approach was to ensure the pupil knew exactly what he had done wrong and why it was wrong. The staff most certainly did not adopt 'the teacher is always right' attitude. That this approach worked was brought home to me one day when dealing with a particularly trouble-some pupil. He was in difficulties, not for the first time, with two of his specialised subject teachers. When I pointed out almost in total exasperation the string of negative reports I was getting from members of staff, the pupil looked at me wide-eyed and said in all innocence, 'It's not fair Sir, that you get all the shit'.

The less able pupil

The question of the pupils' perception of themselves is a very impor-tant issue. In a highly-structured organisation, like a school, where teachers have so many pressures on them for results. Teachers may have to 'push' children in order to draw out the best of the pupil's talent. But faced with reluctant, noisy pupils, it becomes difficult to maintain a positive approach. How many teachers at the end of the day can recall praising pupils as opposed to shouting and generally criticising them? This was brought home to me once when discussing a pupil, 'Paul', with a colleague.

Paul was fourteen years old, small, underweight and unable to read.

He was disruptive in class and rarely out of trouble. I identified his educational weakness and developed some low-key approaches to help him. But on top of that I let him know that I was concerned. I encouraged him, I praised his slow success and almost immediately his disruptive behaviour was greatly reduced. When analysing his improvement I decided that it was probably one of the few times Paul had received positive encouragement. This is not to say that there is a magical approach that instantly transforms the less able into paragons of virtue.

Of course, what works with one pupil will not necessarily work with another. In a class of eighteen there are eighteen separate individuals with separate needs, wants and desires. How teachers cope with them on both the collective and individual basis will depend on so many variable factors that no teacher can possibly prepare or plan for.

Some less able pupils are attention seekers, perhaps the joker of the class, playing tricks, making rude noises at crucial moments in a lesson. Some are talkative, always giving the answer without being asked and always trying to divert the teacher into talking about something other than the business in hand. On these occasions, particularly if the teacher is a good talker and/or actor, the class will be totally absorbed. In understanding pupils these moments are invaluable for the teacher, for it is then that the pupils begin to reveal hidden aspects of themselves in the resulting discussion. However, then there are the quiet ones. These lads can be just as big a problem as the disrupters.

'A culture of silence'

Once the children become used to a teacher they seem to feel no need to actively 'resist' the teacher. Is this what Friere (1972) called the 'culture of silence'? The less able are a major part of a 'dispossessed class'. Few of my pupils had a parent in employment: those that did tended towards manual labour or occasionally a mother worked as a cleaner in one of the local schools. Friere postulated the belief that ignorance and apathy were the direct product of a whole situation of economic, social and political domination and of the paternalism of which they the dispossessed were the victims. The values and cultural attitudes of teachers are not those of the dispossessed. Consequently in the classroom pupils can erect a wall of indifference. It has taken me many years to recognise that indifference and the lack of ambition are direct products of powerlessness. As Hopson and Scally

(1981) say, 'they are depowered'. Hopson and Scally indicate four reasons for depowerment:

1. as a consequence of early learning;
2. as a consequence of the social group we are born into;
3. because political groups and governments typically hide information from people making them dependent;
4. because professional groups' main priorities are to maintain their privileged position by ensuring that people will depend on them.

The less able certainly have had early learning experiences that have reinforced their belief in their own 'stupidity'. One pupil 'James' was extremely weak at reading. When he realised that the concern and interest of the teaching staff was genuine he began to seek ways of improving. In praising James I introduced him to a new feeling. For once in his life James was not in his own eyes a failure.

During all my years of teaching I've never had a less able middle-class child. They do exist but not in the catchment area of our school. There is sufficient evidence in education to establish a co-relation between membership of a low socio-economic group, feelings of powerlessness and low educational achievement.

Hopson and Scally's third reason for deliberate depowerment is a controversial one in the context of west Belfast. On one occasion in the mid-70s a project involving youth workers and four schools was developed to encourage a meeting of less able pupils from both boys and girls schools in the area. The pupils were encouraged to meet informally in a controlled situation to explore their own values and attitudes. The project was stopped by 'clerical interference': that which cannot be tightly controlled, cannot be tolerated. Of course nowadays with 'education for loving' and 'education for mutual understanding', such contacts are encouraged.

On another occasion as part of an Irish history course I displayed British educational material from the Jackdaw series on the 1916 Irish Uprising. It was one of few educational topics that seemed to activate the pupils for they saw its relevance to the world around them. Mind you they knew little of Pearse and Connolly or Carson and Craig. The display provoked angry comments from British soldiers during a raid on the school one night. This led the headmaster to ask me to justify the display of the material on educational grounds.

Outside the classroom

General school policy was that the 'troubles' should be kept outside the classroom. With the abolition of corporal punishment teachers have new opportunities to show other alternatives to violence without being hypocritical. Certainly the abolition of corporal punishment has removed the fear of beatings from many less able pupils for indeed, they suffered the most. But whilst we try to create a haven of peace inside the school it is not always possible. Clashes have occurred between pupils going to and from schools and soldiers. It's one of the facts of life in west Belfast.

Some of the pupils have viewed the situation in a different way from those in authority. Pupils often compare experiences of riots. But it would be wrong to see in this any political motivation in a sense of understanding issues or knowing why things are happening. Most are unaware but simply 'know' who the enemy is and respond accordingly. The less able tend to become the most active participants in whatever riot is occurring. They take the lead in hijacking and in burning buses and cars, partially for the excitement and partially for the sense of importance it gives them within the community. The same is one who has had a life of failure and rejection and whose leisure activities whether of glue sniffing or Friday night wine drinking in the City Cemetery usually meet with community rejection. Some boys can find the occasional tacit community approval for rioting a welcome change.

There is of course a negative effect. One pupil caught up in a bomb blast adopted an attitude of almost total withdrawal. He rarely communicated with his class mates, had few friends and spent his home time in his bedroom watching television. His work was usually good but he lacked social skills. How he and the many others emotionally damaged by the troubles will cope, only time will tell.

I was always conscious that at the end of the school day I could go away from the area and its problems. My pupils could not. They remain in the Whiterock.

Lack of motivation

The less able pupils have needs and interests of their own. For example, they need adventure or excitement to combat boredom; rioting or joy riding provides that. Joy riding is a major problem in west Belfast. A number of my ex-pupils have been joy riders and several have been killed. Not all the joy riders in schools can be easily identified. On the contrary they are as likely to be as quiet, hard-working pupils as the next. It is usually only through classroom gossip that I can identify the joy riders. Naturally enough the teaching staff have tried to re-educate the pupils involved but not always with great success. Mostly they are involved for the excitement, for the thrill of doing a 'hand-breaker' and a chase. Occasionally some are involved for profit, stealing the cars, wrecking them, then selling them for scrap. My most attentive classes have usually been when we have discussed the morality of this and the insurance implications of people who drive their cars up to barricades or riots and ask the youngsters there to burn the car! When they see the double standards of some adults, is it any wonder that the youngsters find it difficult to differentiate right from wrong?

Self motivation

In the classroom situation when the teacher has won the confidence of the pupils the boys usually disclose some facts about their life outside school. This usually takes the form of banter whereby the class as a unit discloses information about a pupil in order to belittle or humuliate him. This is one of the most difficult problems to deal with, particularly for the boy, who is the butt of all the jokes and comments. He will be an outsider. Perhaps he smells, perhaps he is the slowest in the class. One pupil I had was a spoiled child at home and immensely unpopular at school. He just didn't get on with the class. He was prone to lying and had many run-ins with teachers. Over a two-year period I worked on him mainly in personal relationships. All attempts proved unsuccessful until, when doing link courses at Belfast College of Technology, he discovered an aptitude for electrical work. His lying ceased, the 1-2 days absences per week stopped. He became well integrated with his fellow pupils, learning to laugh at himself and forming relationships. He now is a reasonably well adjusted adolescent knowing what he wants to do in life.

Another pupil who suffered from deafness was initially a loner in the classroom. He was well mannered, softly spoken but occasionally blew his top in frustration. When we organised football teams he turned out to be an ideal sweeper and his confidence grew immeasurably. We placed him on the one day a week work experience scheme with a local furniture making company. Initially I would go every week to the company checking on the pupil and worrying that his shyness would prevent him from gaining any benefits from the scheme. I need not have worried. Within a month he was an integral part of the workforce sharing in the jokes and banter. Ten years on he is still there, now a part of the management structure in the firm.

Behaviour patterns

Some types of behaviour are developed in the classroom by the less able to protect themselves from ridicule for their failures. In English the class would read a piece of work, I would go through the questions and then ask the pupils to write the answers only. Going around the class there were usually two or more pupils who immediately write out all the questions and would, if there was time, write out the passage as well. They did this simply because of difficulties in reading and under-standing. They didn't know what they were writing but at least it filled the page and that to them was good work. The same tactic is used, of course, in other subjects. Many of the children's answers have been, say, two lines of a passage starting half-way through a sentence and finishing likewise. The pupils also love to copy the book exactly and see lines in books as sentences regardless of full stops and capital letters.

Handwriting can be appalling and many a time the old fashioned Vere Foster handwriting books have helped restore some pride to a pupil's work. A number of pupils write with the pencil tightly gripped, almost fist-like, with their arm above the line and the hand stretching around and down to the line they are writing on. At the same time their bodies are stretched at all angles over the desk. I assume part of this is to prevent the teacher from seeing how poorly they write. In math-ematics anything beyond simple addition and subtraction can cause behaviour problems. It took me some time to realise that some slow workers in the class were not lazy but were unable to read the questions. Hence my initial approach in the class to insist upon each pupil doing all his own work as I had learned in grammar school, created more problems than it solved. I later came to realise when doing careers and life skills that teaching staff in schools were penalising pupils for co-operating whereas in industry and in working life generally it is crucial for workers to co-operate in problem solving. This idea is not always appreciated by some other teachers: they demand and expect absolute silence and strict control in the classroom. With the less able that is what they don't get. The boys talk a lot, move around a lot and exhibit symptoms of boredom and restlessness.

The teacher of the less able

A sense of humour is essential. It can relieve the monotony and routine of life. However, for some authoritarian teachers with a heavy emphasis on rules, discipline and covering the syllabus, teaching the less able can be an uphill battle of wills as each side tries to dominate the other. A lot of conflict situations arise when less able boys and authoritarian teachers meet. Pupils work better when they are happy. Being able to laugh with the pupils and also being able to laugh at oneself can be an extremely important factor in motivating the pupils. Pupils will give respect to a teacher whom they can both laugh with and work for. He knows his job, teaches them something and shows that he has human qualities.

Another important quality is flexibility. A class straggling back after a swimming lesson and coming in in dribs and drabs can disrupt the best prepared lesson. Therefore, the teacher needs to be flexible. Some of my best lessons have been totally spontaneous and involved all the class in discussion of some issue. At other times realising that the subject was boring I've stopped the lesson and perhaps quickly organised some leisure activity. Also the pupils enjoy leaving the school for trips. Certainly for the less able these trips can be an important educational experience.

Perhaps the most crucial quality a teacher of the less able should have is the ability to respect the pupils as people. I've realised it is not my subject that I teach but the pupils. In other words emphasis is placed on the pupils rather than on the content of the subject. This is crucial to establishing a stable working relationship with the less able and that relationship can be the key to creating the correct conditions whereby the less able may begin to learn. Praising positive and ignoring negative behaviour whilst extremely hard assists greatly in establishing the necessary relationship. Children hate to be ignored. In many cases disruptive behaviour is their cry for recognition. It gets the teacher's and the class's attention and that may be the only attention they get in their lives. Whenever my pupils know the rules I have found that unacceptable behaviour can be controlled easily by not recognising the pupil. In most cases the pupils will very quickly modify their behaviour and seek once more to be recognised in and by the class.

It can be difficult but teachers must distinguish between the pupil and his non-acceptable behaviour. We condemn the action but not the pupil. After all the less able fourth/fifth year pupil will be leaving school in a relatively short period of time. He will thus have completed ten or eleven years of compulsory education. During that time he has invariably been labelled a failure, his self-esteem is low and he may well have acquired a reputation as a troublemaker. No matter how hard teachers try not to, we are all still influenced to some extent by word-of-mouth reputation – a pupil may have a reputation even before a teacher meets him. Knowing that this happens, I have tried to ensure that the pupils know at the start of the year they have a clean sheet, at least with me. The previous year's misdemeanours are forgotten. It is now up to them to begin to take some control and responsibility for their own lives. As I often say to them, if they don't take responsibility for themselves and like themselves why should they expect anyone else to either like them or take responsibility for them? That is something they do understand. However, it can at times be very difficult to maintain a positive attitude and respect for the pupils. There are some pupils who are so obnoxious that they would try the patience of a saint. Some pupils can think up numerous strategies to disrupt class. They can pass wind, belch, drop pencils, fire catapults, steal other pupil's possessions, 'lose' their books, take 30 minutes to write a sentence while simultaneously slagging some other pupil's parents.

I judge success by the development of socially well adjusted pupils. I try to ensure that they have the social skills to enable them to survive in the world. So in school we emphasise good manners, politeness and respect. These are virtues valued by parents, by employers and by teachers. They are virtues valued by the pupils. That the pupils recognise this is success in itself.

Conclusion

The less able pupils because of their social, economic and educational disadvantages are entitled to better resources than they currently enjoy. They can recognise their disadvantages and their subsequent low esteem thus reinforcing a sense of failure. Teachers who empathise with pupils will develop a positive relationship that can create the conditions for learning. In this context discipline will come from the pupils and not the teachers. Teachers of less able pupils should be teachers of pupils before being teachers of subjects.

In west Belfast processes of 'depowerment' have exacerbated the problems of the less able. Social problems such as joy riding can be attractive alternatives to those who feel, and who society views as, failures. However, teachers can have a positive role to play in their day-to-day interaction with pupils. Armed with a sense of humour, an open mind, a flexible approach and an ability to recognise the worth of every child the teacher is likely to assist children in the learning process. And surely that's the least the less able has the right to expect.

Chapter 8

Managing a Small Primary School

Emma Caul
(Principal, Bruslee Primary School, Newtownabbey)

Introduction

Michelle's mother has finally decided to transfer her to another school. For Bruslee Primary School this could spell disaster. Michelle, a less able and, to say the least, a difficult child, is going to a large, though more convenient, primary school. Michelle's loss represents a 6% drop in my enrolment. That's 6 pupils in a school of 100 or 12 in one of 200 pupils. Yet there's not time to worry about Michelle, we both (the assistant teacher and I) ask, will she cope in the new school? Can she climb stairs? Will she make new friends easily? Will she be moved again to a special school? However, there's the roll to mark, P7's number work to be checked, transport to be organised for a school trip to the pantomime, a student is coming in soon and I must find out when, the computer needs fixing I really must take it to Ballymena today (Board headquarters) 'Yes Emma' . . . (P7 pupil).

This chapter looks at the management of a small primary school and illustrates the dynamics of working with small numbers. The account describes the environment of the school and sets the process of managing the curriculum into perspective. In particular the problems of being a teaching principal are illustrated in a school within a selective context. The school is continually striving for its very existence as gradual rationalisation erodes the educational fabric of the rural community in this area.

The school and its environment

Bruslee Primary School is situated on the main road running between Belfast and Larne. The area is known for the council tip, a large, partly-filled quarry across the road from the school. The village is small, running along both sides of the main road, and contains in addition to the school, a shop, a garage and a church hall. No more than 40 people live in Bruslee. The school serves the village and the surrounding area, one of relatively prosperous mixed farms. Few children come from the village itself and are brought to school by parents. The decline in the number of families involved in agriculture on a full-time basis adds pressure to the struggle to keep the enrolment at a level that would sustain a two-teacher school. With parents travelling to employment in Ballyclare, Larne and Belfast, it is easier to send children to schools in those locations than to the local school. Also when older children transfer to secondary school it is simpler for parents to make one school run to the secondary school in Ballyclare and to send younger children to primary school there also. However, this school is well supported by an active parents' group which has rallied to the school's assistance on a number of occasions. A tradition exists that local people attend Brusles school. The present school was extended in 1956 as a result of local rationalisation and a merger with a small 'country' school. Nevertheless falling numbers due to a lack of a given catchment area and the changes in the pattern of employment locally have resulted in a fall in numbers from 48 pupils in 1982 to 22 (1989). Bruslee Primary School will have one teacher in 1989/90.

The school is managed by the North Eastern Education and Library Board (NEELB) although it has its own board of governors. The governors comprise two local councillors, two parents, the assistant teacher and representatives of the local churches. However, control of the curriculum remains highly centralised and is the preserve of the Department of Education whose inspectorate carry out local evaluations and advise on educational policy.

Primary education is selective and culminates with an 11+ test for transfer to secondary school. Since 1980 the system of transfer has been based on attributable testing. While the Department tinkers, almost on an annual basis, with the naming of grades and with percentages the non-standardised tests are administered annually. The inconvenience of constantly changing administrative requirements only adds slight irritations to the annual demands of practising and rehearsing past papers. Once the P7's tests are over, P6's drill begins.

Central policy regarding small schools is contained in the Demographic Trends document (DENI, 1982) in which it is argued that schools of less than 100 pupils in rural situations are not viable. This rather arbitrary measure defines the four-teacher school as the minimum unit of effectiveness. Is Bruslee, by definition, not an effective school? However, the Board does have a policy of rationalisation which is clear and does take account of local circumstances. The North

Eastern Board believes that it can sustain two-teacher schools but not a one-teacher unit. If a school's enrolment falls below 26 pupils, inevitable closure follows. Bruslee Primary School has a life expectancy of around one further academic year.

The local Board encourages curriculum development. I have had parapetetic support in music, physical education and drama. Although on an arbitrary basis the assistance of and the arrival of a new face helped. Science and maths have become areas of concern. This year a maths specialist worked with my class; P5, 6 and 7 groups on a Monday morning. However, since 1983/84 NICED Guidelines have systematically posed questions about the curriculum. I attended a Board seminar in March 1984 which launched the initiative in schools in this area. With neighbouring schools my assistant and I have discussed our aims and objectives, a policy for language development and health education. This year I have begun to collaborate with two researchers looking at problem-solving with young children. We have just acquired a third computer which is proving invaluable and helps develop the children's confidence in microelectronics.

Since 1980 the curriculum of the school has changed dramatically. We have introduced a considerable emphasis on group work and I use the children's natural organising ability to 'effect' their basic work. The P5–7s use the time from 9 a.m. to 10.45 a.m. to work individually through a range of set work including oral reading, number work, comprehension, tables and composition. At the same time I check learning and written homework. The children have become much more process orientated and can get excited about finding out about issues and events.

NICED Guidelines articulate the issues in each school discipline and would help a school tease out many relevant aspects; however, the demands of the total curriculum are, in a school, much greater than any one part. It is the change in the children's learning that is significant not the systematic consideration of subjects.

Bruslee Primary School has become much more open in its approach over the last decade. The school has student teachers on a regular basis, hosts a research project and welcomes any support that the Board will provide. I have managed the school's expenditure since 1983 on a 'consolidated allowance' schedule which allows the school to use any savings on a year's expenditure on additional equipment. Both rooms have improved in this regard over the years.

Teaching in Bruslee Primary School

This year there are twelve pupils in the P5-7 class, less than a half of my 1981/82 numbers. Two children are in P5, three in P6 and seven in P7. The present P7 class now numbers 50% of its 1983/84 size. The class consists of two brothers, a brother and sister and three first cousins. One family is engaged in full-time farming, four families work on the land in a part-time capacity, one family has a pet shop while one parent is a teacher at a local secondary school. The children, while living in relatively isolated farms, attend one of two churches and their youth organisations. The children find initial co-operative activities in group work difficult. They are, however, naturally inquisitive and keen to find out about what is going on.

The P7 group divides into two types of child. In the one group Paul, Emma, Lynne and Sara are able, bright and inquiring children. Peter, however, although not dull, is an under-achiever who has interpersonal problems, particularly with adults. The other boy, Paul, is enthusiastic, challenging and physically big but less able academically than the other children. Tracy, on the other hand, while less able is quiet and reserved.

Two of the three children in P6 are slow academically, while Elaine, an ardent equestrian exponent, is among the more able pupils to have attained Bruslee. In P5 Stephen is able but quiet and Carolyn a sister of 'big' Paul is more able than her brother. Educationally the children need stimulation and new challenges. They work well in relatively unsupervised groups and can organise their work adequately. Challenges must be set at the level of each child and reflect the ability of the children to work capably on their own. However, a relatively isolated background is not without its advantages. Many of the children read avidly and most are creative and imaginative in drama, play, writing and art work. What the children lack in not being 'street-wise' they compensate for in being self-contained and in resourcefulness.

This is my fourth school in a teaching career of 24 years. It is my second promoted post having been head of infants at a large urban estate school. Large becomes a relative concept while at Bruslee. When I came to Bruslee I taught the P4-7 class while in my earlier career I worked with infants. The change was not as traumatic as I expected, however, I was taken aback for a while by the capacity of the children to organise their own work. The constant need to supervise children, in my other schools, gave way to a less disciplined approach although some of the bigger boys tried it on at first; children as they say, never change.

I found my administrative roles strange at the beginning but I soon settled into a routine where the running of the school is integral to my working day. The greatest change I encountered was how to handle the composite class. My infant experience stood me in good stead and I quickly adapted group work to the demands of the older pupils. Most of the children's work is completed in groups. Their self-reliance and enterprise helps when their work is completed. When their work is marked they continue to work quietly without having to be told to do so. The reading corner and the computers are invaluable resources. I learnt quickly that I had to plan ahead and organise my set work on a group basis. Each child works through a sequence of work, sometimes sharing their work and ideas with other children. If you think ahead it is the obvious thing to do. When I remember my 'whole class teaching' in other schools I wonder how I managed to hold everyone's attention for so long. Or did I?

When I came to Bruslee at first I noticed the rural aspects of the work. The children read brochures about tractors and farm machinery, judged the quality of a good cow and kept pet sheep. Many still do so, but I don't notice that interest any more. It's just an aspect of working with rural children. However, it is a country community and if I don't remark on it as much today, the tradition of being happy at school, parental support and community identity is still as strong as it was when I came in 1980. There is a strong expectation about perceived success in the selection procedure. Parents want their children to go to the grammar school. It's a 'social thing' with many parents; ability and an aptitude for the pace of life at such schools doesn't really influence their thinking. Those children we think will get a non-fee-paying place normally do so. I honestly cannot remember a child who I thought 'grammar school material' not getting a place. Although in 1983/84 some parents took children away from the school for various reasons and some of those children did not do as well as I would have predicted in the selection tests.

Bruslee Primary School was extended in 1956 to accommodate a school rationalisation. In 1981/82 a staff room was added and the toilet block incorporated within the fabric of the school building. The school has been gradually re-equipped since 1980 and a range of audio-visual and electronic equipment is used. I use three micro-computers on a daily basis. Unlike some of the neighbouring schools Bruslee has a playground and play area, although the use of a field at the back of the school was lost in 1982/83.

When I came to Bruslee I was concerned initially with my role as an administrator. I was unable to 'stand back' and take stock of the kind of education the school was providing. I had clear ideas about the quality of school in some specific aspects. The reading scheme was sets of Ladybird books and I immediately set about changing to a more contemporary one. My approach to the teaching of mathematics was made more process orientated than that used previously at the school. Maths had to become more about understanding than pure computation. However teaching and administration had to be integrated in a working day.

The following diary sets out my work with Primary 5–7 (8–11 year-olds) over a period of a week, 5 days in the life of Bruslee Primary School.

MARCH 1989

20 MONDAY

9.00–9.05	Children give birthday cards and present to student (it was her 21st on Saturday).
9.05	Back to class. Go over English with each group in turn – take till 9.40. By this time there are children waiting for help with some of their work.
9.40	Start reading with first group.
10.05	Have heard all the groups. Between times I have marked several children's work and helped others with difficulty.
10.20	Coffee arrived 10 minutes ago. No time to drink it – it's cold 'yuk!' Most children have finished English and are ready to begin maths – only 4 children still working. Some of those who have finished are working at computers – 'Colony' – a problem-solving game.
10.25	Play Bingo game with children who have finished English.
10.45	Everyone finished English. Go out for break. Pile of books to mark. Tuck shop money to check. Need TV for broadcast after break.
11.00	TV Programme 'Zig-Zag' – about co-operation in the animal kingdom.
11.20	Discuss the programme – how the same co-operation occurs in human life, e.g. how do we co-operate in the making and distribution of cornflakes?
11.35	Begin maths: P7 revision of decimals; P6 introduction of 24-hour clock; P5 working out how long things last using time line. (Carolyn has great difficulty. I need to work through it with her at her desk.)
12.00	Lunch time – 3 children not finished maths – Carolyn is struggling – needs more practice.

LUNCH   Stack of mail arrived at break. Need to go through it:
1. Ulster Branch – Irish Hockey Union – Northern Bank Mini Hockey Championship.
2. Royal Mail – Young Letter Writers' Competition.
3. NI Committee of the British Field Sports Society – province-wide poster competition and literature about visits to Shane's Castle.
4. Catalogue – Stanley Thornes & Hulton.
5. Catalogue – Nelson – Peak Maths.
6. Catalogue – Hamish Hamilton Children's Books.
7. Books from Ward Lock Education for Inspection – 'The Now Project'. Still helping children with maths.

12.15	Write up homework on board.
12.20	Mark books.
12.25	Go to staffroom for lunch.
1.00	Back from lunch – go over homework.
1.10	Handwriting.
1.30	Science – experiment into the stretchiness of wool.
2.20	Remember to switch on tape-recorder to record 'Sciencescope' for later in week.
2.30	Notice that only a few people had taken milk. Had to send children out for milk – had to send message into Ethel (assistant teacher) to get her to ask her class to drink theirs as well.
2.40	Read next episode of novel.
2.55	Get children to role play a scene from the story.
3.00	Children go home. Fill in roll book and daily record book as well as FMI for milk.
3.10	Finish marking. Put TV and radio away and switch off computers.
3.15	Quick chat with Ethel about student and her plans for the remainder of her teaching practice.
3.25	Preparation for tomorrow.
3.40	Finished for day.

March 21 Tuesday

8.45	Met at door by children wanting discs for the computer. Take a few minutes to look at the books that arrived yesterday. Need to find a story for assembly.
8.55	Phone call from Peter's mum. He will be in later. He is kicking up a fuss at home – his dad will bring him. Elaine and Jennifer (P6) come to explain they could not find 'pried' in the dictionary for homework last night.
9.00	Ring bell and give out hymn books. Get ready to go to assembly.
9.15	Student not here yet (will she or won't she come?). Spelling and tables. Peter still not here (P7).
9.30	Strange phone call. Young lady asked if it was Bruslee PS then the line went dead.

9.35	Begin English and reading. Need to go round each group in turn.
9.45	Library service left 4 books written by Diene.
10.35	Peter arrives.
10.45	Break. Pile of books to be marked. Mail is in. Will try and get it cleared by 11.00.
	Letter from DENI – Commonwealth Day Message 1989.
11.00	Radio broadcast – 'Time and Tune'.
11.20	Broadcast over – have to get TV to record programme at 11.40. Set maths: P5 time lines – need to sit with Carolyn; P6 24-hour clock they can work alone; P7 revision of decimals – need to go through it then they can work alone.
11.50	Ethel came in to say that student left to have her car fixed.
12.00	Stop children for lunch. Stephen, Paul and Peter have work to finish. Write homework on board.
12.05	Mark last night's homework. Make out worksheet for P5 for tonight. Stop and rewind the video.
12.15	Go for lunch.
1.00	Go over tomorrow's homework. Watch 'How We Used To Live'. Discussion of problems of living in high-rise flats.
2.00	P7 back in for craft. Making woven pencil cases – this has kept them busy for about 4 weeks so far.
2.10	P5 and 6 go into Ethel (assistant teacher) for craft. P7 stay outside clearing litter blown into the playground during storm last week.
2.20	P7 want to rearrange desks so that they can all sit at one table together. They discuss the arrangements as they work.
2.30	Jennifer came in to borrow the 'fluorescent' pink paint.
2.40	Elaine asked to borrow red paint.
3.00	Children go home. Need to undo tacking on Lynne's pencil case – now she has finished that, I must get her something new for next day. Time for preparation for tomorrow and filling in daily report book and roll book. It was Peter's birthday today – perhaps he was reluctant to come to school because he feared the 'bumps' more than the table test.

March 22 Wednesday

9.00	Give out spelling and table books. Must hurry today. Swimming at 10.00. Go over English with each group.
9.20	Phone call – Paul answered. Had to leave P6. Phone call to say new photocopier to be delivered today. Need to have table or desk ready to set it on.
9.30	Ethel came in with roll book. Iris Woods (Principal) of Millbrook asked her to apply in 'trawl' for new post.
9.40	Spelling and tables.
9.45	Mark English.

9.50	Begin reading.
10.10	Time to leave for swimming – still have to hear one more group for reading. Must remember the money for entrance to the pool.
10.10	Just on my way out when salesman phoned. He tried to sell me software for computer.
10.15	Leave for swimming.
11.30	Back from swimming. Set maths for all groups. Hear last group reading.
11.45	Do some marking. Get it cleared for lunch-time. Mail has arrived. Carolyn (P5) still having trouble with time-lines. Spend 3 separate short sessions with her (3–4 mins per session). Peter and Paul both write £40 as £0.40 when working out what change they would get from £40 if they spend £36.91.
12.00	Children leave for lunch. Time to mark yesterday's homework and put up homework for tomorrow.
12.20	Mail. 1. Brochure about computer software. 2. Details of BBC (Ulster) TV and radio broadcasts for next year – order forms.
12.25	Lunch at last.
1.00	Go over homework. Check milk. Send table to staffroom for computer. Check corrections, etc. Give out Lucky/Chip Club forms.
1.15	Handwriting practice.
1.45	Drama.
2.05	Phone call from Ward Lock Educational Books. Query about outstanding account for books on inspection 31/5/87. Books had been returned in September '87. Account for £51.65.
2.15	Men arrive with new photocopier.
2.20	Play a quick number Bingo game.
2.30	Children leave for music with Ethel. Time to prepare for tomorrow and fill out daily record book.
2.31	Man who installed photocopier came to show me how the new machine works.
2.50	Lesson over – back to work. Need to note the names of the children who did not go swimming for a refund at end of term.
3.20	All work done. Need to leave now. University at 4.00. Caretaker has not arrived yet. I cannot leave till she comes because her children are here and there is no-one to look after them (Ethel is at computer node).

March 23 Thursday

8.55	Arrived late – snow. Ethel gave report of computer node. Possibility of computer table if I put in requisition immediately.
9.00	Children come in – they want to stay out in the snow. Sara's dad has made a shelf to hold the computer.

9.05 One group spelling.

9.10 RE broadcast 'Together'.

9.30 English, spelling, tables. Work with each group in turn.

9.50 Remember to switch recorder on for broadcast.

10.15 Reading groups.

10.45 Stop for break. Still need to hear one group read. Try to get Victor McCabe (Computers) twice on phone but line engaged. Do some marking. Need to get TV to record broadcast at 11.20. Radio broadcast to be recorded at 11.40.

11.00 Break over. Jennifer in tears. Paul hit her on the face with a snowball. Takes 5 mins to settle the dispute. Go over maths. Carolyn still struggling with clocks and how long something lasts.

11.20 Set video to record. Hear last reading group. Mark maths as it is completed.

11.40 Set radio to record. Work through worksheet on volcanoes with group. Filling in labels on a cross-section and finding volcanoes in various parts of the world.

12.00 Not finished but we must stop for lunch. Try to get Victor again. Had a long chat with him. He is doing B.Ed. Hons course too. He is in Year 2. Need to write up homework.
Mail.
1. Invoice from UTV for pamphlets.
2. Mailing from NAHT.

12.30 Go for lunch – have to make a worksheet for P5 maths homework.

1.00 Back from lunch. Need to make sure the milk is taken. Children take down homework and I go over it.

1.15 Watch TV programme recorded this morning – a programme about earthquakes and volcanoes. Need to ring Xerox service – switch on new machine faulty. Engaged.

1.40 Programme finished. Ring Xerox again – still engaged. Number games.

2.05 P5 & P6 go to Mrs Logan for craft. Try Xerox again – got through – engineer to come out to look. P6 continue with craft. Lynne has finished weaving. Must find her something else to do.

2.10 Tried out a new computer programme 'The Fleet Street Phantom'. Children joined in while weaving.

3.00 Still at game. It is very good but children need to go. Caretaker not her at 3.10. She is supposed to start at 2.55 at latest although I asked her to start at 2.00. Her time keeping is dreadful.

3.15 Usual book work and preparation. Phoned County Hall purchasing to inquire if they had extra computer trolleys. They did not. Tried Carol Steen (NEELB) – engaged.

3.30 Carol Steen phoned back – spoke about position of school ref. staffing. She will be out Monday 13 March 1989.

3.35 Spoke to caretaker about time keeping.

3.40	Phone call from Anne Reid, Personnel Department, County Hall. She wanted to speak to Ethel about her request for early retirement.
3.50	Time to go home.

MARCH 24 FRIDAY

9.00	Spelling and tables.
9.05	Les arrives (Bob) (College lecturer to work with the computer).
9.20	Begin work on 'Bob'.
9.35	Mrs G arrives (University researcher). More work on 'Bob'.
10.45	Break.
11.00	Break over. Work on 'Bob'.
11.20	Student goes home – ill.
11.30	Les leaves.
11.40	Mrs G leaves.
12.00	Lunch. Children want to make Mother's Day card for Mrs Vennard.
1.00	Lunch over. Try to get noticeboards organised for Tuesday. Children make Mother's Day cards and finish flowers.
2.30	Children go to Mrs Logan. I try to clear chaos. Mail.

1. Inspection copies of books from Gill and Macmillan.
2. Invitation to table quiz at Ballyclare PS.
3. Catalogues from Hodder and Stoughton.
4. Voting papers for election of vice president NAHT.
5. Poster from VLC for Easter club.
6. Mailing from County Hall.
   a. Notice from Mr Leadley about availability of plants from the Garden Centre Carrickfergus.
   b. Appliction for Curriculum Support teachers for 1989/90.
7. Time sheet returned – not completed by lunar months – rude notes from some beaurocrat attached – 'bugger them'.

Although a working day appears cluttered and confused, the reality is a busy job which doesn't allow time for much thought. However, a teaching day does have a sense of purpose and meaning beyond the normal interaction between teacher and pupil. Throughout all the telephone calls and interruptions to the classroom routines, I'm still the children's teacher. I must talk with any number of people from county advisors to salesmen who come to the school each day. Nevertheless, the work in the classroom continues unabated. It is not a priority, it is the essence of the school; it is where learning occurs and I'm not the central resource in the learning situation.

In compiling my diary I found 110 items worthy of recording in a week's teaching. Of the events recorded less than 20% or 22% involved working with children. I wonder what's it like in a 'big school'. Was I regularly removed from the children by telephones and the demands of colleagues when I taught in a school of 400 pupils?

If curriculum is an all embracing term for those aspects that contribute to the process of teaching and learning then the 'ad-curriculum' may described how a teaching principal organises and works throughout a school day. The process is rational, even if the events of a day indicate otherwise.

It involves a process of planning ahead and organising children's work so that scope will exist for all those activities essential for managing the school. You can either make things easier for yourself by planning or leave things in a disorganised heap for another day and be overtaken by the next crisis. It is essential in my experience to build a day around a curricular pattern that is flexible enough to cope with an ongoing procession of people who will interrupt the teaching. However, the running of the school does not hinder or indeed interfere with the learning situation as it is this that is integral to the smooth running of the school. Teaching in a small school takes on further dimensions and incorporates a range of activities that are necessary if the teaching itself is to continue unabated.

While selection at eleven is an important part of my work, it does not, nor can it, overshadow the rest of the curriculum. For the sake of the P7 children it does take precedence in September, October and November of the school year. It is a part of primary education and while it remains so it is my responsibility to work within the system. However, all small schools live under the shadow of declining enrolments and possible rationalisation. Selection tests are a ready reckoner for the local community. Closure almost stares schools in the face when numbers fall below 30 pupils. Then it is a matter of time before the numbers reach the low 20s and as Board Advisers say, schools then just close themselves. Once the spectre of closure appears rumours spread rapidly among the local community. Then the rate of decline only multiplies and falling enrolments intensify to hasten closure. It looks now as if I will be busy for just one more year.

'Yes Emma?'

Chapter 9

Youthways: Training 'At Risk' Adolescents

Dermot McCartan

(Development Officer, Regional Curriculum Base, Jordanstown)

The age of the unemployed teenage consumer

High levels of unemployment among 16–19 year-olds became a feature of the mid and early 1970s. As traditional and often outmoded working practices gave way to the new technologies, those areas of the country, in particular urban inner-city areas, that had for so long depended on this traditional pattern of labour suffered the brunt of change. The combination of new technologies and the irresistible competition posed by vastly cheaper imported goods from the Far East in particular caused established sources of employment in the Northern Ireland region to go into a sharp decline. In addition to Belfast areas such as East Antrim, Derry and the north-west which had to a large extent come to depend on one or two major industrial sectors such as tobacco, chemicals or textiles, felt the draught of unemployment as large employers, many of them multinationals established on the wave of the 1960s economic boom, left the province.

In the climate of shrinking job opportunities those young people who left school with qualifications or visible evidence of attainment were better placed to enter the world of work while the rest became in the words of one Labour politician of the time 'dole fodder'.

Between March 1974 and September 1976 the number of wholly unemployed school leavers in Northern Ireland had risen dramatically from just over 1000 to well in excess of 9000 and there was growing concern that those who were unable to gain employment through lack of qualifications, appeared equally unable to progress to some form of training or meaningful alternative to their unemployed status. An added twist to the problem was that surveys had shown that the turnover of labour in the employment patterns of the 16–19 year-old age group was unusually large, apparently demonstrating the ill-preparedness of many young people for the world of work thus causing them to stay in jobs for only a short while.

The response

It was against this background in March 1976 that the Department of Education for Northern Ireland (DENI) set up a working party to examine the unemployment problem among young people and to investigate the feasibility of establishing programmes which would cater for their needs. Disturbing evidence had also indicated that the problems of unemployed youth went much deeper than merely suffering the frustration and stigma of the accompanying status; their experiences during the last year or two of compulsory education and their failure to get a job and thus make the 'normal transition' to adult life, had in many instances left them disenchanted with the educational system in particular, and with society in general. It appeared that lack of opportunities in the spheres of social and vocational education led to young people remaining gauche, bereft of self-confidence, poor in communication and interpersonal skills and generally unrealistic in their perceptions of the world of work. The greatest concern in this continuum of isolation was that young people would reach the stage of 'dropping-out' of a society in which they felt they had little stake and in which the degree of control over their own lives was marginal.

The DENI working party recommended that special courses should be designed and implemented to cater for those young people in greatest need of support: the aims of such programmes would be the raising of the young people's self-confidence and self-belief, helping them to relate to society in general in a more positive way, and overall to make them a much more attractive proposition to potential employers than previously had been the case. Initially each course was to last 14 weeks and would have a complement of 25 young people and 4 course tutors, the courses themselves adopting the name 'Youthways'.

The philosophy

Following DENI's acceptance of the working party recommendations, a panel was created to devise programme content. Although this panel was drawn mainly from the DENI Inspectorate it also included representatives from other Departments including the then Manpower Services, Health and Social Services and Agriculture. Representatives from the Southern and Western Education and Library Boards completed the membership of the design panel, since it had been decided to locate the first two Youthways pilot courses in these Board

areas. The pilots were to implement, pioneer and test this new educational initiative for unemployed youth and resultant developments
were to be monitored and analysed by the Central Economics Service
of the Department of Finance.

In January 1977 two pilot courses were started in Craigavon and
Derry with the following objectives:

> To demonstrate and test an experimental learning programme for
> young unemployed as a preparation for employment and living.
> To evaluate its effectiveness and so provide a set of adaptable
> structured learning exercises capable of being integrated into
> schools, industry and employment service programmes.
>
> (DENI, 1977)

These successful pilot programmes led to the establishment of a
detailed course framework augmented by a wide range of component
learning materials to be used on future courses. The guidance manual
for Youthways tutors, which was still in the process of being drafted was
to state:

> Within the overall framework of the courses tutors are free to
> devise by judicious selection from those detailed notes, schemes of
> work based on the identified needs of the young people on their
> courses.   (Youthways Staff Manual)

This new approach was to emphasise the importance of each individual
young person on Youthways courses and tutors were advised to tailor
the learning programmes in a flexible way to reflect particular interests,
aptitudes and needs of each individual. Tutors were further advised to
adopt 'imaginative and innovatory approaches in their teaching and
general dealings with the young people' (Youthways Staff Manual) and
by so doing would hopefully cause the young people to be stimulated
and motivated in a much more positive way than their recent experiences had dictated.

The philosophy and format of Youthways certainly seemed to appeal
to the young people to whom the courses were aimed. They seemed to
value the realistic approaches which the tutors offered. There were no
attempts to structure learning experiences around theoretical subjects
or areas of work which demanded involvement in the formal education
system. Indeed as Youthways courses became available throughout all
five Board Areas in Northern Ireland the temptation towards FE
college integration was resisted and the Youthways locations became
college out-centres, and by design, self-contained units of operation.

Personal development underpinned the whole basis of Youthways: it permeated and found expression in the general aims of Youthways courses and in course content and organisation generally. Even until the present day the aims of Youthways have changed little, rather the actual course organisation and emphasis may have developed in response to changing external social, economic or vocational factors. I became part of a Youthways team during the era of expanding provision at the end of the 1970s with youth unemployment still climbing steeply towards the 13 000 mark. My introduction was the first-week residential/induction phase of the course which I found, I must confess, a daunting and intense experience. Yet I had felt challenged and confronted by many group issues that week. This deep and often heavy group experience of the residential week was, in the view of most Youthways tutors, an indispensable part of the whole mutual learning process and usually culminates in the evolution of a set of group agreements or a signed contract between course members and tutors. It was also a generally held view that the working through of problems and issues which leads to the contract itself was a unique bonding process for all involved and that anyone who did not wish to take part in the residential/induction week, without reasonable justi-fication, should not be considered for the course itself. It is also during this week, as often as not in the various social, informal settings which the residential offers, that meaningful and sometimes significant personal relationships between tutors/students were built.

Thereafter, the typical Youthways week was composed of two plenary group days and three work placement days. This pattern continued throughout most courses interrupted only by the detachment/outdoor pursuits week (usually between the 8th/10th week of the course) or other specific or individualised course elements such as a period of community action.

Youthways and the Youth Training Programme

At the start of the 1980s, in addition to Youthways courses, provision for the young unemployed continued to expand in response to the still escalating unemployment figures, (just under 15 000 in 1981) under the general umbrella of the Youth Opportunities Programme. This broadening and often disparate spectrum of provision was in dire need of rationalisation, and in 1982 the Departments of Manpower Services and Education addressed this problem with an initiative known as the

Youth Training Programme in Northern Ireland. As well as restating the original rationale of Youthways *et al*, the definitive document stated:

> In recent years it has become increasingly clear that the vocational education and training of young people must be provided in a much more comprehensive and systematic fashion than has so far been the case.
> (DENI, 1982/15)

School leavers at age 16 without jobs, were to receive the offer of a 'Guaranteed Year' i.e. 'the offer of a guaranteed minimum of twelve months consecutive vocational preparations'.

Both Departments who were to jointly manage the programme, clearly envisaged Youthways as having an important part to play in the new arrangements and went on to suggest that:

> the successful YOP Youthways courses aimed at the least qualified groups will be incorporated as a foundation module in the programme.
> (DENI, 1982/15)

The rationale of Youthways courses was to remain valid but the inclusion of the courses in broader YTP demanded that staff planned provision in the light of these aims (DENI, Circular 1982/15). The thematic approach suggested by YTP was in fact extremely compatible with the Youthways experience which had always put strong emphasis on the curriculum framework being delivered through such themes as negotiation, guidance and counselling. It was notable that following the advent of YTP in September 1982, Youthways still endeavoured to see the most disadvantaged young people as its specific target group: research carried out on the pilot courses had shown that 40% of the course participants had also to cope with problems of a physical, educational, mental or social nature, and it now appeared that this trend was to continue. In my experience, it was precisely those kinds of young people who benefited most from the programmes, in that they felt much less marginalised and much more self-confident, through the psychological 'space' which the course gave and the refusal of the tutors to expect them to conform.

Since it appeared that Youthways courses were to enter into partnership arrangements with other course providers in an integrated 'Guaranteed Year' structure for each young person who so desired, then staff obviously had to look at the degree and depth of learning experiences and probable total time contributed to each of the three now common elements – Vocational Training, Work Experience and Further Education – by all the modules comprising the young people's

Guaranteed Year Provision. It is fair to say that most Youthways tutors would have concurred with the Departments' sentiments in their introductory document to YTP which envisaged Youthways as a 'foundation module'. It must also be said that the introduction of this planned framework was never pursued with any conviction by those responsible for implementing YTP/Partnership Arrangements and where it was attempted, it was done so in such a desultory fashion as to inhibit further experimentation thereafter. Many of the careers staff who were responsible for placing school leavers in the various types of provision that were on offer, were either unaware of the existence of Youthways courses or were not sufficiently *au fait* with their principles or philosophy to enable them to advise participation on the part of the young people. Also, as with any efforts at effecting partnerships, the co-operations involved and the ability of all the partners to see benefits in new arrangements must be prerequisite, and, in my opinion, neither of these conditions were sufficiently in evidence to induce any sort of meaningful allegiances in any of the courses of which I have had experience.

Youthways still continued, however, to be attractive as a course in its own right and still managed to occupy, despite wholesale restructuring all around it, a somewhat unique position in the YTP constellation. It still did not fit easily into either of the twin camps of education and training. In some ways it could be said that the failure of the partnership philosophy worked in favour of the chances of success of subsequent Youthways courses in that it was still the experience of staff – who were nonetheless prepared to participate in an integrated structure – that young people who came on Youthways courses following a period of unemployment adapted more successfully and reaped more benefits from their programmes, than those who entered directly after leaving full-time education. I always felt there was a marked difference in response and attitude from those who took part in the second course of any given year: they would have tended to demonstrate a level of maturity of response not consistent with the slight age differential from those on the first course, and an almost total absence of initial suspicion that Youthways was 'more of the same' i.e. schooling and formal education. The corollary to that was of course that by then their level of 'street wisdom' and knowledge of 'the system' had increased dramatically and in this respect would have suggested a different set of problems and concomitant strategies than their first course counterparts. It was therefore obvious that Youthways courses were becoming increasingly important in fulfilling dual roles, at different times of the year. The first course was seen basically as providing a foundation module for succeeding parts of YTP while the second has provided opportunities for those who had not found suitable provision to date, or who had been reluctant to engage in, or had dropped out of, alternative types of schemes.

I feel that perhaps one of the strengths of the Youthways philosophy, and one reason why it has continued to appeal to young people, has been this inbuilt ability to mould itself around the various needs and aspirations of its different client groups. The apparent loose structure and total informality of approach to which course members will readily relate, will usually hide, however, a high degree of advance planning, experience of adolescent psychology (mainly practical!) and a genuine desire to stimulate and motivate response from the young people through giving them a real negotiating and decision-making role. For example, it is likely much of the recreation/leisure elements of any course will be decided and organised by the students themselves: also, work experience/placement aspects of their own particular programme will be arrived at through the negotiations process, since this is a particularly good example of an area of young people's lives where they would quickly reject the notion of other people – no matter how well-intentioned – taking important decisions on their behalf.

A further innovative and challenging spin-off derived from the experiences of Youthways programmes was the development of courses known as 'Routeways'. Designed to respond to certain suggestions contained in the Warnock Report (1978) which looked at special educational needs and intended generally to create provision 'for unemployed but potentially employable young people in the ESN (on) range, age 16+' (Warnock, 1978) these courses were almost a mirror image of Youthways with slight differences in curriculum content, student ratios, etc. The main difference was in fact the length of the course – Routeways would run for 34 weeks with 7 integrated phases – but in other respects, tutors were quite happy to adopt the good practices already developed by Youthways particularly in the areas of aims (a direct restatement of Youthways), course structure and philosophy, tutor/student relationships, etc.

Aims of Youthways courses

As the programme has been devised to meet the needs of the unemployed young people who are unqualified, untrained and unmotivated the general aims of the Youthways courses are:

1. to be directly relevant to the needs of the young people as future workers, students or in continuing unemployment;
2. to provide the young people with purposeful and interesting activities which demonstrate that each of them can usefully participate in some particular sector of employment and in society at large and which are helpful, therefore, in mitigating past or present disadvantage whether it be social, economic or educational;
3. to enable the young people to gain a more realistic assessment of their abilities and aptitudes and so adopt a more positive attitude towards life and work;
4. to help the young people make more realistic and informed choices about jobs or other opportunities open to them;
5. to develop the young people's skills and knowledge which they require to move competently and confidently in the various personal and group encounters that are part of everyday life;
6. to improve, extend and diversify their capacity to communicate and be communicated with;
7. to develop their literacy and numeracy skills;
8. to enhance their ability to find and compete for suitable jobs;
9. to improve their capacity while out of work to cope with the pressures of unemployment in a positive and constructive manner;
10. to enhance their understanding of the economic, industrial/commercial, political, social and environmental factors which affect their lives;
11. to improve their capacity to cope with the many and diverse personal problems that can arise in their lives;
12. to help them develop their powers of creativity and initiative whether at work or at leisure;
13. to develop within the young people a greater sense of responsibility in their own actions and future; and
14. to encourage greater sensitivity and responsibility in their personal relationships with their elders, peers, juniors and the opposite sex.

Structure and organisation of Youthways courses

COURSE DESIGN

The Youthways Course Programme has been devised in the light of certain constraints. In the first place the young people will not be motivated by the idea of continuing formal educational especially if it is seen by them as 'more of the same'. Activities which will have greater appeal for them will be those of a practical nature. However, most of the young people will have already taken in school some practical subjects such as woodwork, metalwork and typewriting but in many cases they will have become disenchanted even with such practical experiences as these because of their inability to master the craft skills involved and so achieve satisfying levels of attainment. Nevertheless a programme based on theoretical subjects or academic work of quite modest demands would be even less likely to succeed.

The core of the programme is planned as a range of practical activities wider in scope than anything the young people may have experienced previously but no more demanding on their aptitudes and abilities than those which they could reasonably be expected to manage. The practical activities fall into two main categories. First, those concerned with the world of work and intended to give the young people some useful skills and greatly broaden their knowledge of the range of jobs available to them. Second, the young people are introduced to a wide range of leisure pursuits to show them new ways of using their free time.

The young people's appreciation of jobs open to them and their individual role in society is enhanced by gaining some insight into how industry, commerce and society in general are organised. Accordingly the programme provides for some instruction in industrial and environmental studies. It must be emphasised that this instruction should arise as naturally as possible out of practical activities and must not be dealt with in a formal and traditional classroom situation. The planning and presentation of such instruction, which must be very relevant, may well be more difficult and require to be more carefully devised than is normally the case.

The young people's self-confidence and their ability to cope with the personal encounters of everyday life depend greatly on their communication skills. The programme also provides, therefore, for work on the literacy, numeracy and general communication skills needed by them. This work can contribute much to the young people's personal development provided it arises out of their typical life experiences, is based on clearly relevant material and is taught in a sensitive and sympathetic manner.

COURSE CONTENT

The major components of the course are:

1. Skills and Practices, which provide practical experience in performing tasks in various sectors of employment and give some insight into the basic skills and working environment associated with particular jobs.
2. Industrial and Environmental Studies, which deal with the structure of various sectors of industry, commerce and social service, their occupational groups and the roles of their separate undertakings in society, together with related environmental studies.
3. Communication Studies, which cover appropriate oral, written and graphical communication and numeracy essential for coping with the demands of particular jobs and in society at large.
4. General Activities which comprise a wide spectrum of leisure pursuits.
5. Personal Development is an integral part of all aspects of the courses. Throughout their entire programme of activities relating to work or leisure the young people should have opportunities to revalue their past experiences, gain new skills and, by a realistic assessment of their true potential through meaningful achievement, gain increased confidence in themselves.

With the exception of the Induction and Detachment weeks (for reasons apparent below) Monday to Friday of each week should be based in the course centre and used for discussion sessions, briefing and debriefing, some work on the studies content of the programme and general activities. The other three days of each week are to be spent on job sampling, skills development, related studies and work experience. The course should run from 9.00 a.m. to 5.00 p.m. each day.

COURSE ORGANISATION

The course is divided into five phases which have particular contributions to make to the overall development of the scheme.
   The phases and their duration are:

   Phase 1   Induction – Week 1 (Residential)
   Phase 2   Sampling – Weeks 2 and 3
   Phase 3   Development – Weeks 4 to 7
   Phase 4   Detachment – Week 8 (Residential)
   Phase 5   Placement/Project Work – Weeks 9 to 14

Youthways assessed

Throughout the whole development and establishment of Youthways courses (and indeed of YTP generally) a major concern of tutors and college management has been the need for appraisal and evaluation of the overall aims and practices that underpin the philosophy – issues such as course content and objectives, tutor techniques and strategies, etc. Course tutors had been asked to adopt a number of broad-based elements of a personal development and vocational nature, and through their own styles and approaches to ensure the effective and coherent delivery of these elements in a combined programme. Specific aspects of trainees response and progress in certain areas may have been measurable – e.g. the acquisition of new vocational skills or technologies – but there was a greater concern about whether or not the emphasis overall was in the right direction, and whether or not objectives were being realised. This in itself posed another problem in that tutors were never quite certain that course objectives as set matched the expectations of course members. This is not intended as a self-criticism; rather it is a testament as to how perceptions varied as to the strengths of the programme. During the personal interview session of the induction/residential week, when asked as to their reasons for joining Youthways the vast majority of young people replied that, from what they had heard, 'Youthways gets you a job'.

Of course, Youthways tutors were always quick to point out that anyone who had moved into full-time employment through Youthways did so on their own merits and that all the course could hope to do was to offer the work placement and opportunity for young people to demonstrate and express their talents. By taking this line of reasoning tutors were able to emphasise the preparation and activity required on the part of the students themselves in order to develop the necessary armoury of skills to assist in the difficult and highly competitive search for the elusive conditions known as 'employability', and eventually employment itself. Simultaneously the opportunity was presented to tutors – while hopefully occasioning this proper and adequate social and vocational preparation – to satisfy some of the course objectives which they themselves had set for the students – i.e. the acquisition of decision-taking skills, planning skills, etc, the possession and utilisation of which would be of life-long benefit, and which would be transferable into a variety of contexts and situations. In recent years, the efficacy and validity of the response of Youthways since its inception, both in achieving its objectives and satisfying the needs of the young people whom it seeks to influence, has been examined in a number of studies which set out to assess the impact of YTP generally. Notable among these have been *Are They Being Served?* (Whyte,

Kilpatrick and McIlheney, 1985) and *The Youth Training Programme in 5 colleges 1983–1984* (1985).

The former study was undertaken on the initiative of the NICER and partly funded by the Department of Economic Development who were obviously interested to see how YTP was viewed by staff and young people alike. The duration of the project was two years – August 1983 to July 1985 – and the research team stated its terms of reference thus: 'to investigate the implementation of the Guaranteed Year Curriculum in YTP. To obtain and assess participants' reaction to the curriculum in the shorter and longer term'. With regard to specific courses such as Youthways it sought in particular to establish, among other things, the extent to which the course content appeared relevant and appropriate, and addressed 'the stated or perceived needs of the trainees'. The response of these programmes was also analysed to determine the degree of opportunity there was for young people to sample a broad range of skills. Certain course practices were also examined to see if the necessary support mechanisms, such as guidance, counselling and appraisal, were facilitated. The study showed a broad and wide-ranging picture of the relative strengths and possible shortcomings of total YTP provision: it is interesting to isolate references to Youthways and to briefly mention some of the conclusions reached by the authors. They believe for example (p. 119) that 'the objectives of the course as stated by their tutors were being translated into practice' (Whyte, J. and McCartney, R., 1985).

The qualification 'as stated by the tutors' is of note, since the authors also make reference, on a number of occasions, to the fact that all Youthways young people were not happy with this emphasis and felt that

> the vocational skills they were learning were related to their job aspirations to a lesser extent than trainees on other courses.
>
> (Whyte, J. and McCartney, R., 1985)

Despite the fact that Youthways students were also felt to be better able to integrate their in-centre curriculum content to the work experience element, these findings would suggest that staff and some students were still approaching experiential situations from very different reference points. However, it appeared that Youthways' students felt more satisfied and expressed more positive views about their course than did most other YTP young people to the extent that 75% of those interviewed said they would advise school leavers to join Youthways.

The DENI survey was similar in purpose to *Are they Being Served?* but as the title implies, limited its scope to YTP in five specific FE colleges. Satisfaction with the general success of Youthways programmes is expressed on two fronts:

the ability of tutors to integrate programmes and individual/group needs, and

in maintaining learning themes within a framework of broad course aims.

In addition, reference is made to the high degree of student-centred activity within the Youthways format, while also echoing *Are They Being Served?*, by suggesting that a greater focus on vocational skills training in the process of enhancement of personal effectiveness was needed. The good practice developed on Youthways courses, the survey suggests, particularly in tutor/student relationships and the student-centred approach to learning, could be adopted in other YTP provision.

Given the breakdown of the week for a typical Youthways course, three days work experience plus two in-centre, I find it hard to see how the so-called 'vocational skills element' be extended as the above surveys suggest without prejudicing the other developmental and learning situations facilitated by the in-centre group and individual programme would argue that three full days out of five is quite sufficient to devote to any one aspect of course provision.

The staff

The non-traditional, innovatory and variety-of-strategy approaches in working with young people, so favoured by the whole Youthways rationale, obviously implies certain beliefs and attitudes on the part of the tutors themselves. Tutors may come from a variety of backgrounds – teaching, youth work or industry – and may be further selected for their ability to complement the skills of the other two tutors in the team. It would also be reasonable to assume that the area of expertise of a particular tutor would reflect the demands of his/her role: it is unlikely, therefore, that two tutors whose specialist skills lay in the outward-bound/outdoor pursuits field, for example, would be found in one team, while it would also be unusual to find this type of person employed for that particular expertise alone. Ideally tutors would bring a range and combination of skills and expertise such as those above to bear in their dealings with young people but it is also important that the right balance within the team is sought. The day-to-day demands which the job imposes on a tutor will be slightly daunting and disorientating initially, in that the tutor may well be unsure what he/she actually is – teacher, youth worker, counsellor/advisor. The range and depth of relationships that a tutor must deal with on a regular basis in the course of this job – youth, employers, college authorities, various statutory bodies, etc. – will necessitate the possession or development of well-honed sets of interpersonal and communication skills. A good deal of administration is also necessary, particularly for the senior course tutor, who will also be responsible, albeit unofficially, for the performance of the ancillary staff.

Overall, the job of a tutor is much more demanding and varied than might at first be assumed and would certainly not appeal to those who have been used to the cocoon of a timetable, or the 'cells and bells' of traditional teaching settings. Further demands on the flexibility and adaptability of staff are imposed by the high value placed on residential experiences (four per year in total) which are usually intense in themselves, and also the amount of work undertaken outside 'normal hours' in the form of home liaison, or simply student counselling.

In addition, the Youthways team tutors are encouraged to be openly and constantly both self-evaluative and peer-evaluative so that the best working practices and strategies are being matched to each individual situation. Good teams are, in my opinion, characterised by this ongoing analysis of performance – in its basic form it would take the form of 'checking out' or debriefing at the end of particular in-centre sessions, to gain immediate impressions and assessments of how they had gone, possibly with the view to shaping further actions or strategies. This spirit of openness, while useful in breaking down possible wrong assumptions or inaccuracies of individual tutor perceptions, also imposes certain behavioural demands and responsibilities on each team member which in many cases may be hard to cope with. Not everyone is equally comfortable or adept either at giving or receiving advice or criticism no matter how well-intentioned or constructive it may be.

Recruitment of students to any particular course may still continue through the informal networks which tutors have established – youth clubs, probation service, even parish bulletins – as much as through the regular channels of the careers service, past-student recommendations, etc. Many of the young people recruited in this fashion would have been 'referrals' particularly where there was collaboration with probation officers. Such young people would generally have been placed in the Youthways situation because it was felt that the structure and philosophy of the course would help in the process of keeping these young offenders out of trouble while simultaneously helping them make more constructive use of their time. Typically, the course tutors would be particularly keen to see positive outcomes in such cases, hopefully in the form of some type of employment at the end of the course. Many tutors have gone to court to give character references and reports of course progress in such cases and the exposure to a programme such as Youthways would have been seen by all involved as valuable support in preventing the cycle of re-offending from becoming established.

While Youthways staff have accepted the need for a committed, innovative and stylised approach to their job certain negative side effects of the nature of the job have also become apparent which pose certain important questions for the recruitment and continuing personal and professional development of staff.

The continual use of residential experiences, groupwork situations, the high degree of interpersonal dealings with students, who often brought varying degrees of delinquency or criminal activity to the course, combined with the *ex officio* duties which tutors were expected to perform were all considered to occasion the incidence of stress among staff. So much so that tutors were advised to spend no longer than five years in Youthways in order to pre-empt the 'burn-out' syndrome. However, this very issue in itself would bring complications, both of a practical and perceptual nature. It would be no easy accomplishment to slot Youthways staff nicely into mainstream college arrangements, even if certain departments were able to absorb extra personnel there would be no guarantee that Youthways staff would be able to teach the subjects required. There has been also, from the early days of Youthways provision, a certain amount of tension evident between Youthways and main college staff stemming from the fact that the latter were often quite unsure what role Youthways played in the educational spectrum of the college. Consequently Youthways tutors were regarded as 'educational entertainers'.

The misreading and misunderstanding of many of the signs and trappings of Youthways provision, e.g. the intentional casual dress of tutors, informality of relationships, the use of a visible strategy such as outdoor pursuits to deliver a subliminal message – have no doubt contributed to this scenario while at the same time causing a certain amount of resentment amongst Youthways staff that some of their colleagues were slower than others to recognise the educational and interpersonal/social potency of such approaches.

Initially the fact of being located in the semi-autonomy of an out-centre was seen by tutors as advantageous in that there was a high degree of control over their programmes and physical environment. For the students there was also the benefit of the feeling of personal 'space', the possession of their own facilities away from the possibly intimidating backdrop of the college itself. (Research with some of my own students in fact had shown that they were quite pleased to be associated with certain college-based courses, such as basic computer studies or hairdressing, on a 'link' basis but would not have been over enthusiastic about an extended college experience.)

Over the years however, I have found that staff have become increasingly divided as to the wisdom of such a philosophy. Those who began to question the prevailing arrangements did so on two main counts:

(i) They considered it unwise to 'condition' the young people on their courses into remaining aloof from the educational system, and had come now to believe that colleges were sufficiently informal and 'user-friendly' in themselves to warrant an increased level of participation from Youthways students.

(ii) Secondly, and more importantly from their personal and professional development and career point of view, staff came increasingly to the view that out-centres of any description were seen by colleagues as educational backwaters and that as far as promotion, responsibility and generally being 'in-the-know' was concerned, then out of sight was certainly out of mind. It was felt to be relatively easier to raise and maintain a higher profile the nearer one was to the general office.

A survey and review of all Youthways courses and tutors throughout Northern Ireland was instituted by the Regional Curriculum Base (RCB) at the University of Ulster at Jordanstown and completed in the autumn of 1988. The purpose and objectives of the review entitled *Youthways: A Staff Development Review* (1988) were generally stated thus:

> . . . to determine the extent of staff development needs expressed by Youthways tutors and also to determine to what extent those needs could be applied to other tutors engaged in YTP courses in general.   (Youthways, 1988)

The study is wide-ranging, looking at staff profiles as well as analysing needs and represents probably the first major study of tutors' perceptions, views and recommendations. As well as RCB staff, there were also five Youthways tutors on the review team and a representative of the DENI Inspectorate.

The document is quite comprehensive and makes extremely interesting reading: the conclusions would certainly reflect some of the concerns to which I have alluded. For example reference is made, on a number of occasions, to the high stress and low morale factors experienced by staff culminating in danger of '5 year burn-out'.

> Current opinion would indicate that staff have to deal with increased levels of deviant and disruptive behaviour, as well as deep-seated lack of motivation on the part of many Youthways participants.   (Youthways, 1988)

It was also interesting that the feelings of mainstream college staff were generally unaware of the roles practised and difficulties experienced by Youthways staff. The report also goes on to recommend that local management 'take a more constructive approach to (all) these issues' and 'take greater cognisance of the concern of Youthways tutors in relation to their career plans. Some efforts should be made to discuss the generally felt frustrations of staff over lack of belonging to the college as a whole' (Youthways, 1988). The report also makes the point that although generally Youthways staff are a well-qualified cohort (e.g. within the group with one to six years Youthways experience, 85% are graduates) they are expected to deal in a multi-faceted roles and responsibilities scenario with over 1000 young people per year in total, and that no induction process exists for new tutors. The absence of a structured staff development plan is also remarked upon.

The one-year Youthways

Regular in-depth review and evaluation of course practices and philosophy has led many Youthways tutors to question the continued use of the arbitrary sixteen-week course structure which had always been the accepted norm. This seemed to stem from an increasing belief that a restructured course, possibly extended over one year, would not only have greater benefits for staff and students alike, but would also allay the sense of frustration and disappointment felt at the untimely breaking of relationships. The sixteen-week format was also becoming disjunctive with other considerations such as FE link provision, progression to grant-aided employment such as Workscheme (where the young person must be of a minimum age to qualify), longer-term individual development such as literacy/numeracy tutorial work, etc.

Several courses adopted this one-year format and have subsequently reported greater satisfaction for all concerned. Tutors point to improved development in particular areas such as:

> The building and bonding of student/tutor relationships and opportunities for increased personal development.

> Project work and individual programmes undertaken – these were now much more realistic and structured to allow for proper execution and completion.

> Assessment for both tutor and student benefit, in that formative assessment of student progress and performance appeared now to be more meaningful and integrated also that students were now able to gain a much more realistic and extended impression of their working environment and personal career performance and potential over one year, not based on short-term or seasonal considerations.

> Continuance and enhancement of motivation and performance of young people, which might have been expected to flag once their course ended.

From a purely logistical point of view tutors who had piloted the one-year programmes were more inclined to suggest their adoption on a permanent basis. Considerations such as the need to recruit students just once per year with one basic induction phase, the organisation of one pool of employers and other course links to facilitate this one student group, and longer-term planning opportunities offered good reasons to find the one-year format more attractive.

Much of the nature and structure of YTP implementation has also changed and it appears that Youthways has become increasingly self-standing as the training situation around it continues to change.

Conclusion

This chapter has traced the philosophy and development of Youthways programmes from inception up until the present time. It has also demonstrated the ever-changing and dynamic nature of total youth training provision generally in Northern Ireland and how Youthways in some instances has had to adapt reluctantly to these changes, e.g. by moving from the original sixteen-week format to the yearly model.

Young people will always respond positively to sympathetic and understanding adults using innovative and imaginative strategies.

PART III

Issues Facing Schools in Northern Ireland

Chapter 10

Education within a Selective System

Anne E. Sutherland
(Research Fellow, NICER, Belfast)

Introduction

As soon as selection began in Northern Ireland there were complaints that it was having a detrimental effect on the primary curriculum. Criticisms have followed the changing pattern of testing; when mathematics and English played an important part, the tests were seen as imposing a straitjacket on these areas; when the emphasis was on verbal reasoning, there were allegations that schools spent undue time giving coaching in the special skills involved. In a situation in which the DENI apparently approves a maximum of eight hours of special preparation but does not or cannot prevent schools from doing more, rumours of excessive coaching abound.

The 'Transfer Procedure Project' broke new ground in attempting to obtain systematic evidence on the effects of the Transfer tests on the curriculum. Some popular beliefs were supported. Though a few schools adhered to the DENI's advice of minimal coaching, most teachers admitted to doing more and some to doing a lot more. In one of the eight selective schools in the Sixteen Schools Study Transfer dominated curriculum for a year, leaving the pupils too jaded to benefit from the remainder of the P7 year; the teachers expressed regret but felt obliged to conform to their perceptions of parental demands. Although the stereotype of the '11+ dominated' school has a basis in reality, another important finding was the range of times spent on coaching.

The Sixteen Schools Study, however, also suggested that the Transfer Procedure may sometimes serve as a scapegoat for all curriculum ills. Despite protests that Transfer was holding back curriculum development, the schools that were more free of Transfer were not necessarily seriously involved in the implementation of the NICED Guidelines or other modern approaches and, indeed, the school which had had no candidates for three years spent longer on English and mathematics than was recommended in the Ministry of Education's 1956 *Programme for Primary Schools*.

It appears less useful to talk about the primary curriculum being distorted by selection than to think of it as being shaped by a number of forces – some competing, some collaborating – of which Transfer is one. Simply removing selection tests is no guarantee of any great curricular improvement.

At secondary level the effect of selection in the bipartite system is an increasingly polarised curriculum over the years of compulsory schooling, even for pupils of similar ability. For the M-grade pupils the differences were most marked in foreign languages, technology and, though to a lesser extent, in science.

Implementation of the framework described in 'The Way Forward' would entail, at both the primary and secondary stages, a widening of the curriculum in many schools.

At the primary level it will be of interest to see whether the balanced curriculum as envisaged becomes a reality or whether, in the next stage of adaptation to a selective system, some schools will concentrate only on the examined subjects. At the secondary stage it is being questioned whether the continuation of a bipartite system is compatible with a common framework or even if both elements can survive.

Selection in Northern Ireland, 1948–89

Selective secondary education was established on a province-wide scale by the 1947 Education Act (NI). Before then most pupils attended elementary schools until age 14. A minority received an academic education in a grammar school but in the mid-1940s only 3% of the age group were awarded scholarships (ACE, 1971).

Over the years different procedures have been used to select pupils for grammar schools. Between 1948 and 1965 there was a Qualifying Examination with tests in English, arithmetic and intelligence. Though Wrigley (ACE, 1955; ACE, 1960) showed the intelligence tests to be good predictors of later academic success, the tests in English and arithmetic, which were based on the syllabus then prescribed for all primary schools (Ministry of Education, 1932, 1956), were the chief determinants of qualification. The intelligence tests were used mainly for border-zone pupils and to screen under-age candidates.

Criticisms were soon heard. In a Stormont debate in the very month of the first qualifying examination, April 1948, there were accusations that the standard of the tests was unreasonably high, while the Minister himself mentioned rumours of excessive cramming, including special classes at night. The following year the Advisory Council for Education was given a special brief to investigate the extent of undue preparation for the qualifying examination. Its 1952 report could only recommend constant dissuasion of 'cramming' through circulars, press notices and the Inspectorate; the hope was expressed that the building of more secondary intermediate schools would reduce the pressure on grammar schools. The Fourth Advisory Council (1960) deplored the payment of fees to professional coaches and the exploitation of parents by commercial publishers but admitted ignorance of the extent of these practices; they also found it impossible to obtain positive evidence supporting allegations that the qualifying examination narrowed the primary curriculum or caused severe pupil stress on any scale.

By contrast, the Fifth Advisory Council (1964) was led by the written and oral evidence it received of pupil stress and 'undesirable backwash effects upon the primary school curriculum' to recommend that the Qualifying Examination should be replaced by a Selection Procedure. This used a combination of scores on two verbal reasoning tests and scaled teacher estimates of suitability for a grammar school education and lasted from 1966 to 1977. It was hoped that the change would encourage a more experimental and broader curriculum (Ministry of Education, 1966).

Though there were now no syllabus-based tests, the Seventh Advisory Council heard accounts of excessive coaching for the verbal reasoning tests in some schools but did not know how widespread this was. Their 1971 report reviewed the existing evidence on coaching, which suggested that effects on performance varied in extent and even in direction for different children, and concluded that if pupils, parents and teachers could not co-operate in confining coaching to agreed limits, the selection methods would be so subject to distortion as to be invalid. The limited amount of preparation they recommended – the administration of one practice test and three one-hour sessions of coaching before each of the main tests – was the same as had appeared in a Ministry Circular (1967/55) accompanying the issue of a specimen test. The circular, which roundly condemned excessive coaching as unprofessional conduct, was re-issued annually until 1977 and, since it has never been rescinded, it still officially stands.

In 1973 the Advisory Committee recommended in the *Burges Report* that selection at eleven should cease, though a minority report, with four signatures, argued the case for retaining voluntary grammar schools. The majority recommendation was publicly accepted in June

1977 by the then Minister of State in the Labour governemnt. In what was intended as an interim arrangement pending reorganisation, an Alternative Transfer Procedure was set up. On the basis of their top year group's performance in non-attributable tests, primary principals were each given a quota to use in allocating pupils into categories of suitability for different types of secondary education. This system survived for only three years, from 1978–79 to 1980–81. One difficulty it faced was that many principals nominated more pupils for grammar schools than their quotas permitted. Changes each year in the subjects of the comparability tests, in the degree of central supervision and in the nomenclature and percentage distribution of the categories brought little credit or credibility to the new procedure. There were particularly vociferous complaints from teachers over the use of mathematics and English tests in 1978, for which a syllabus was demanded, and in 1979 a verbal reasoning test was substituted on the grounds that it would lead to less distortion of the curriculum.

After the Conservative victory in May 1979, plans for secondary reorganisation were shelved and priority given to re-establishing a stable selection system. Following consultation, there was a return to attributable testing. Each autumn since then there have been two tests 'of the verbal reasoning type with some questions designed to test aspects of English and mathematics'.

Between 1980–81 and 1986–87, and including the time of the NICER Transfer Procedure Project fieldwork, the top 20% in the age group were awarded an A grade, which entitled them to a non-feepaying place in a grammar school. The next 10% were awarded an M grade: if selected by a grammar school (though this was not guaranteed) they were non-feepayers. All remaining candidates were given a G grade and could be admitted to a grammar school only as feepayers. In 1987–88 a simpler system was introduced whereby 27% of the age group were awarded non-feepaying places. Boys and girls were treated as separate populations until a High Court verdict in the summer of 1988 declared that this practice contravened the Sex Discrimination Order (NI) 1976 (see Gallagher, 1989).

Approximately 10% of Northern Ireland secondary pupils are in systems that do not involve selection at eleven. In the Craigavon district there are seven junior high schools from which a third of the pupils are selected for senior schools at fourteen. Certain other schools have been designated as non-selective 11–16 or 11–18 schools. Pupils normally transfer to the local junior high or comprehensive school without sitting the tests, though they may be entered if their parents so wish. Conversely, parents in selective areas may withdraw their children from the tests.

Reactions to selection

Meanwhile criticisms of selection continued. There were many lively debates in the Stormont Parliament (see, for example, *Hansard*, 1959, 1963). The critics of selection were, however, divided between those who thought selection wrong on principle and those who criticised only such aspects as the age of testing, the special difficulties of the small rural primary school and the effects on the curriculum.

The mid-1980s witnessed several more or less public statements by the Inspectorate – and on one occasion by the then Under-Secretary of State on evidence from the Inspectorate (Scott, 1985) – regretting that primary schools continued to coach so much. Since 1984 the teacher unions have withdrawn from supervising the Transfer tests and have repeatedly announced their opposition to selection. Sutherland and Gallagher (1986), however, showed rank-and-file teachers to be divided on the principle of selection. While the current method had few uncritical admirers, it was nevertheless preferred to earlier forms. As in a NICER study (Wilson and Spelman, 1977) some nine years earlier, a form of delayed selection was preferred to full 11–16 comprehensivisation.

The NICER studies in primary schools

One of the terms of reference given to the NICER Transfer Procedure was to investigate the effects of selection on the upper primary curriculum. The first study in the series was therefore a questionnaire survey, in February 1985, among the principals and teachers of the two top classes (P6 and P7) in a one-in-four sample of Northern Ireland primary schools. Replies were received from 193 principals and 214 teachers in 199 schools. representing 78% of the schools approached.

The Sixteen Schools Study was based on the premise that the effects of the Transfer Procedure would be more pronounced in selective than in non-selective areas. Only one of the eight 'non-selective' schools had however, no Transfer candidates and in one a majority of the pupils had been entered. The Sixteen Schools Study included interviews with principals and teachers about the curriculum and the completion by P6 and P7 teachers of a checklist of class activities during three separate weeks in the school year, one of which was immediately before the first

Transfer test. In addition, questionnaires were received from 779 pupils and 599 parents.

Throughout the research, Transfer preparation was defined as practice on past or similar tests or as the teaching of techniques for tackling test items.

Because of the DENI's known disapproval of more than a small amount of test preparation there was some doubt as to whether teachers who coached more than the recommended amount, as many were alleged to do, would admit it, especially in a postal questionnaire. It was hoped, however, that the project would, at the very least, help to open up for discussion what had hitherto been something of a 'taboo' area.

Preparation for the tests: the NICER research evidence

Only 6 of the 199 schools participating in the questionnaire survey claimed to spend no longer in preparation for the verbal reasoning tests than the DENI recommends. In over 70% of the schools preparation began in P6 and the amount usually increased as the test dates approached. There was considerable variation in the amount of preparation recorded. According to the principals, just before the tests a fifth of the schools coached for not more than two hours a week but a sixth of the schools spent at least ten hours a week in special preparation, which would be longer than the time given to any other area of the primary curriculum. More coaching was reported from large than from small schools, where Transfer pupils were usually in the same classroom as younger pupils.

Most principals and teachers, especially in selective areas, had felt pressure to increase the amount of coaching, the two most frequently cited sources of pressure being parents (37%) and a belief that other schools spent longer on preparation than they did (49%). These sources were related in that some respondents expressed a fear that dissatisfied parents might remove their children to a school with a reputation for coaching thoroughly. Further analysis revealed that those who feared that other schools coached more than they did tended themselves to do slightly more than average. Anxiety, rumour and over-preparation could operate in an unfortunate cycle.

The Sixteen Schools Study demonstrated more clearly than the survey how special preparation increased to a maximum in the term of the tests (see the penultimate line of Table 10.1). Though the seven non-selective schools with test candidates all felt obliged to provide coaching, such preparation usually began later than in selective areas. In October of P6, exactly a year before the first test, only three schools had begun Transfer preparation. Four months later, in January/February, the average amount of time spent on coaching, in both selective and non-selective areas, was less than that given to music. By June of P6, despite sports days and other end-of-term events, six of the selective schools were engaged in coaching, averaging over two hours a week but only three of the non-selective schools did any. The week before the first test about a fifth of the time in selective schools was spent in direct preparation. That average figure conceals a wide range, from 6% to 51% or from 1.5 hours to 12.75 hours. The very much smaller average time in non-selective schools reflects the difference in the percentages of candidates in the two sectors rather than in the amount of coaching which candidates received.

Two main approaches to organising Transfer preparation were noted in the Sixteen Schools Study. In selective areas most preparation took place in the mornings, when pupils were thought to do their best work, in time previously allocated to English or mathematics. Transfer preparation was, in effect, treated for some months as a third basic subject. In non-selective areas it was commoner to withdraw candidates in the afternoons from subjects such as craft or physical education or to run extra classes outside normal school hours. When all such coaching was included candidates in non-selective areas averaged 4.6 hours a week as compared with 5.6 hours in selective areas.

In the survey the average weekly amount of special preparation reported by teachers in selective areas immediately before the tests emerged consistently as 5.6, 5.1 and 5.6 hours respectively. There was, however, only moderate agreement within the Sixteen Schools Study between the interview and checklist evidence for individual teachers. The discrepancies were in both directions, showing that although some teachers may have tried to minimise their coaching, others exaggerated it. Teachers in the school where there was most coaching seemed genuinely horrified when the amount was added up. There were also indications that some primary principals were not well informed about the amount of coaching their teachers did, which could vary greatly from classroom to classroom, while the teachers were often hazy about when special preparation began in the school. There could be secrecy about coaching not only between schools but also within a staffroom.

Table 10.1   Temporal Variations in Upper Primary Curriculum (time as percentages)

	P6			P7		
	Oct	Jan/ Feb	June	Oct	Jan/ Feb	June
SELECTIVE						
English	28.5	28.8	23.9	22.2	30.6	31.9
Mathematics	20.0	19.2	13.5	13.2	18.6	15.6
Environmental						
Studies	15.5	14.2	16.1	10.0	11.8	14.2
Religious Education	9.6	9.3	8.3	9.8	11.7	8.0
Physical Education	5.2	7.8	10.8	8.3	9.4	14.4
Art	11.2	8.5	9.4	9.8	9.1	7.6
Music	4.0	4.1	5.7	4.2	4.2	4.4
Second Language	0.6	1.0	0.0	0.4	0.8	0.0
Transfer	1.1	3.7	7.3	19.3	0.2	0.0
Other	4.3	3.4	5.0	2.8	3.6	3.9
NON-SELECTIVE						
English	37.7	31.6	23.4	31.5	34.0	25.6
Mathematics	23.1	24.0	17.0	21.5	25.0	15.1
Environmental						
Studies	13.7	13.4	18.0	13.0	13.3	17.9
Religious Education	7.3	10.0	7.9	7.5	9.0	6.5
Physical Education	6.0	5.7	18.4	7.4	5.4	21.9
Art	6.3	6.6	4.6	6.5	7.1	3.2
Music	1.8	2.3	2.8	1.5	2.4	3.7
Second Language	1.1	0.0	0.0	1.2	0.0	0.0
Transfer	0.1	2.0	2.0	5.2	0.0	0.0
Other	2.9	4.4	5.9	4.7	3.8	6.1

(Sixteen Schools Study)

Other effects on the primary curriculum: the survey

Table 10.2 shows how principals saw the effects of the Transfer Procedure increasing over the four upper primary years. Whereas fewer than a tenth saw any effects in P4, nearly two-fifths saw the P6 and nearly two-thirds saw the P7 curriculum as substantially affected. Teachers of P6 pupils recorded greater effects than teachers of younger classes, although only a sixth used the top category. The effects were felt most keenly in large, maintained schools in selective areas but the small group of teachers from the preparatory departments of grammar schools tended to dismiss the effects as 'slight' even though they had recorded an above average amount of coaching early in P7.

In a series of open-ended questions the primary principals and teachers were asked to identify any curriculum area which, as a result of the Transfer Procedure, was over-emphasised, any which was omitted or severely curtailed and any which had benefited.

Mathematics and English, the two subjects most closely related to the Transfer tests, were each considered by about half the sample (56% and 49% respectively) to be given undue prominence because of Transfer. Only 19% and 16% respectively thought these subjects benefited from the extra attention. Though no other recognised primary subject was regarded as either overemphasised or benefiting, 21% replied that verbal reasoning occupied too much time, while 15% saw improvements in problem-solving and 11% in speed and efficiency, which they attributed to Transfer practice.

Two-thirds of the primary principals and teachers pointed to at least one subject area neglected because of the tests and one-third named at least three. The subjects most often identified were environmental studies, science/nature study, history, geography, art and music. Virtually all subjects were mentioned by at least a few respondents, including such aspects of English and mathematics as poetry and practical applications. A small number claimed that everything suffered except what was actually tested. Most respondents (64%) also believed that the implementation of the NICER Primary Guidelines (NICER, 1985ff.) would be impeded because of the Transfer tests, particularly during the P6-P7 years and especially in certain subject areas.

Other effects on the primary curriculum: the Sixteen Schools Study

On the basis of the 1985 survey findings one might expect that, in comparison with the schools in non-selective areas, the eight selective schools in the Sixteen Schools Study would spend longer on mathematics and English at the expense of other subjects, in particular environmental studies, art and music, and that the differences would be most noticeable just before the tests. Table 10.1 shows that this was not the case.

Contrary to expectation, more time was spent on English and mathematics in non-selective than in selective schools, especially in the term of the tests, when the non-selective schools averaged over two hours

Table 10.2   Perceived Effects on the Primary Curriculum (in percentages)

	None	Slight	Quite a lot	A lot
I PRINCIPALS				
in P4	91.5	6.3	1.6	0.5
in P5	67.4	29.5	2.6	0.5
in P6	16.1	44.8	32.3	6.8
in P6	3.1	33.9	30.2	32.3
II TEACHERS				
of P6	14.0	43.0	26.7	16.3
of P7 or P6–7	4.7	37.5	42.2	15.6

more for both curriculum areas. Part of the explanation lies in the tendency in selective areas described above to treat Transfer preparation as a priority subject and to allocate it some of the valued morning hours normally spent on mathematics and English. The non-selective schools, however, also spent more time on mathematics and English early in the P6 year, when there was only a small amount of coaching, and in the term after the tests.

As the survey had suggested, the time spent on environmental studies was reduced just before the tests but, contrary to prediction, art and music were consistently given more attention in selective than in non-selective areas with no noticeable diminution in October of P7. Of the 30 instances where a class did no art or music during the week only one was in a selective area and two teachers in non-selective areas taught no music in any of the weeks of checklist recordings. Evidence of ambitious project work, cross-curricular approaches and involvement in the implementation of the NICER Primary Guidelines were found equally often in both types of school.

It appears that teachers' belief in the relative importance of different subjects is a more powerful influence in shaping the curriculum than the continuation of selection *per se*. In this connection it was noted in the initial interviews that, whatever other education aims and values they might mention, such as fostering enjoyment of learning, self-confidence, or a sense of responsibility in their pupils, all teachers, in selective and non-selective areas alike, stressed the importance of giving the pupils a thorough grounding in literacy and numeracy. In this they had the support of both pupils and parents. Though the pupils' favourite subjects were those with a recreational element, such as physical education, painting, computer work, drama, private reading and educational visits, when they were asked to write down the three most important things to learn at school the vast majority (80% and 78% respectively) named mathematics and English. Their parents were even more emphatic, with 98% and 94% respectively, identifying mathematics and English as among their three priority subjects.

Most parents were ambitious for their children. Only 3% definitely did not wish their child to remain in full-time education after age 16 although a sixth were uncertain, and in selective areas about twice as many hoped for a grammar school place as were likely to get one. Nevertheless, the parents appeared less preoccupied with Transfer coaching than many teachers had suggested. Though two-thirds of the parents in selective areas rated Transfer preparation as 'very important' only 7% nominated it as one of the three most important subjects. In this it ranked below not only mathematics and English but also computer work (19%) and environmental studies (10%).

Though some of the checklist evidence runs counter to the perceptions of the teachers in the questionnaire survey, it resembles the findings of other reports from England (DES, 1978, 1985; Barker Lunn, 1984), Wales (Welsh Office, 1986), Scotland (SED, 1980) and the Republic of Ireland (Burke and Fontes, 1986). These showed traditional teaching approaches, what Blyth (1965) termed the 'elementary' tradition in primary education, persisting well after the ending of selection or, in the case of the South of Ireland, the abolition of the Primary Certificate Examination.

The secondary stage: the curriculum of border-band pupils

Between 1981 and 1985, 73% of the M-grade pupils, who were eligible for but not entitled to non-feepaying places in grammar schools, were enrolled in grammar schools. The percentages ranged from 85% in the Western Board area to only 55% in the South-eastern area (Wilson, 1986). Sutherland and Gallagher (1987) found that in comparison with working-class parents more middle-class parents had applied for a grammar school place (84% vs 59%) and that more of their applications were successful (85% vs 58%) while Livingstone (1987) demonstrated that, as at other Transfer levels, more Protestant than Catholic parents had sought grammar school places but that at this level more Protestants has been disappointed. M-grade pupils, therefore, provide an opportunity to study the experiences and progress of young people of apparently similar ability who find themselves, whether voluntarily or otherwise, in different types of schools.

The NICER Border-band study looked at a sample of 484 M-grade pupils from the first, third and fifth forms of 16 grammar and 14 secondary schools. Table 10.3 summarises the findings of an analysis of the pupils' weekly timetables, with subjects assigned to eleven curriculum areas. Differences between the two types of school increased during the years of compulsory schooling, though in each of the years investigated the grammar school pupils spent longer on languages other than English and on science, while the secondary pupils spent longer on technological and other vocationally oriented subjects. Though the Border-band study examined the timetables only of M-grade pupils, the differences observed would seem to reflect more general differences in the curricular aims of the two sectors.

In first form all M-grade pupils in grammar schools were studying a second 'other' language (which might be Latin) and a quarter of them were taking three languages. In the first form of the Protestant secondary schools French was the only 'other' language taught but in the Catholic secondary schools all M-grade pupils took Irish as well.

In third form the M-grade pupils in grammar schools were usually taking either two or three languages, whereas half of those in secondary schools were studying only one and a few had given up other languages completely. The pupils in grammar schools averaged nearly six as opposed to four periods a week on science and were usually timetabled separately for physics, chemistry and biology, whereas most secondary pupils were still following a general science course. In contrast, whereas almost all secondary boys (97%) studied craft, design and technology (CDT) and the majority were also timetabled for computer studies (71%) and such subjects as technical drawing (79%), the corresponding percentages in grammar schools were respectively 38%, 23% and 11%. A quarter of the secondary girls, but none in grammar schools, had begun commercial studies.

In fifth form the M-grade pupils in grammar schools were typically preparing to sit nine 'O' levels and none was aiming at fewer than seven. Those in secondary schools were more often preparing to sit examinations in between six and eight subjects, of which one or two might be at CSE level. All but one of the grammar schools offered at least three 'other' languages in the fourth and fifth years but half the secondary schools offered only French, which might be available only at CSE level or at the expense of any social science. Conversely, CDT, other technical and commercial subjects were sparsely represented in the grammar school prospectuses.

A general shift was observed in both sectors between first and fifth forms away from langauges, social sciences, physical education and aesthetic subjects towards more science, technology and vocational subjects. Nevertheless, 82% of the grammar school pupils were still studying at least one 'other' language in fifth form and 23% were studying two or more. However, only 31% of those in secondary schools were studying an 'other' language and only 20% were studying a modern European language as required in 'The Way Forward' (DENI, 1988). Some 10% were studying only Irish. Though the percentages that had dropped science altogether were fairly similar in grammar and secondary schools (15% and 17% respectively) more grammar than secondary pupils were studying two or more sciences (55% vs 34%). Chemistry and biology were markedly more popular options in the grammar schools. A technological subject was studied by 69% of the secondary pupils but by only 25% of those in grammar schools. Less than half the fifth-formers from either sector, however, spent any time on art or music. In both sectors the curriculum was narrower than that set out in 'The Way Forward'.

Table 10.3   Percentages of time allocated to subject areas in grammar and secondary schools

Personal and Social Education	1.1	1.4	1.0	2.7	1.4	2.4
Religious Education	6.3	6.3	6.0	6.2	6.7	7.7
Social Studies	14.9	14.4	13.6	14.1	13.0	11.3
English	11.7	13.6	11.6	12.6	14.0	14.5
Other Languages	20.4	14.4	21.3	13.8	11.5	3.5
Mathematics	12.3	12.8	12.1	12.9	15.1	14.3
Science	10.3	8.9	14.2	9.9	19.5	14.8
Technology	2.0	4.1	2.6	6.1	3.4	10.5
Other Vocational	3.9	5.0	4.0	7.5	4.3	8.5
Aesthetic	9.5	11.7	7.4	8.6	4.0	5.4
Physical Education	7.1	7.3	6.0	5.5	4.8	4.9

Effects of selection on performance

In the Border-band study, the 1981 follow-up study (Gallagher, 1988) and an earlier NICER 1975 cohort study (Wilson, 1985) it was found to be academically advantageous, within the selective system, to be enrolled in a grammar school. In each case the grammar school pupils did better at 16+ than would have been predicted on the basis of their 11+ results alone. Gallagher (1988) estimated that across the whole ability range grammar school pupils averaged one third O-levels more than pupils with the same Transfer grade in secondary schools. In the Border-band study the M-grade pupils in grammar schools averaged 5.6 O-level 'passes' (Grades A-C) as compared with 3.8 in secondary schools and they were at a particular advantage in languages and science.

When, however, grammar and secondary schools are treated as the components of a bipartite system and that system is compared with the Craigavon two-tier system and with 11–18 comprehensives, none of the three systems was found to produce consistently superior results at age 18+, if due allowance was made for the ability of entrants (Wilson, 1985). This is a potentially important finding because of the claims sometimes made that the reason for Northern Ireland's A-level results being higher than those from England and Wales is the continuation of selective secondary education.

Within the bipartite system, however, Wilson (1989) argued that the effect of selection is to increase the disparity of performance at the secondary stage, relative to the mainly comprehensive system of England and Wales. Northern Ireland has both more leavers with A-levels and more leavers with no GCE/CSE qualifications and Gallagher (1988) has shown 'unqualified' leaving was at least as common in his admittedly small sample from the Craigavon area and from comprehensive schools as in secondary intermediate schools. Whatever factors lead more Northern Ireland than other pupils to opt out of public examinations would appear to operate beyond as well as within the bipartite system.

Although they are limited in not having analysed the data from different types of school separately (comprehensive, grammar, secondary modern and independent in England; grammar, secondary, Craigavon two-tier and comprehensive in Northern Ireland) the Assessment of Performance Unit (APU) reports of testing between 1978 and 1984 (see Wilson, 1989, for a review) cast interesting sidelights on the effects of selection. The consistently high scores at age 11 in mathematics and to an only slightly less extent in (English) language can be seen as reflecting the thorough grounding in basic subjects given as part of the preparation programme for the Transfer tests (though the Sixteen Schools Study suggested that schools in non-selective areas were equally thorough), while the reasonably good performance in science at age 11, despite a documented neglect of primary science, may be the result of the application of relevant mathematical skills. By contrast, the comparatively poor performance in science at age 15 and the low uptake of science at this stage relative to England and Wales (see also Driver *et al*, 1984) are descriptive of a region where there is full academic provision for only a minority.

Chapter 11

Segregation and Integration in Northern Ireland's Education System

Alex McEwen
(Lecturer, Queens University Belfast)

Introduction

The segregation of schools in Northern Ireland according to religious denomination has a long history and reveals starkly the crisis of identity that exists among the province's people. This occurs because different cultural, ideological and political sources have been used to create and sustain Catholic and Protestant identities: these have respectively Irish and British reference points. As far as schools are concerned, the underlying differences between the two main communities are brought to the surface in the treatment and teaching of school subjects such as history, Irish, sport and to a lesser extent music. In state schools, for example, which are non-denominational but in practice are almost wholly Protestant in ethos, the Irish language is not part of the curriculum. On the other hand, Irish is part of the curriculum of almost all Catholic post-primary schools. The inclusion of Irish in the curriculum is as much a statement about the ethos and cultural orientation of a school – its Irishness – as it is about the need for an additional language either French or Spanish in the school's timetable.

This chapter explores the role of education in transmitting these deep structural inconsistencies of identity. An examination of different aspects of the official curriculum is one way in which this process can be carried out. At the same time, the unofficial or hidden curriculum also translates divergent cultural, economic and political perceptions. These are communicated in schools through friendship patterns which reinforce Catholic or Protestant group identities that by their nature are defensive and present a potentially hostile picture of 'the other side'. The very fact of segregated schooling must also underline the dissimilarities between the two groups and, however unwittingly, contribute to ignorance of and prejudice towards the other community.

The chapter also deals with the alternative to segregation; the development of schools which have been organised along planned integrated lines. The first of these, Lagan College, was established in 1981 and, at the time of writing, a further seven have been created including Hazelwood Integrated Primary School (see Chapter 6) with four more at the planning stage. Part of the present chapter also analyses the apparent discrepancy between the representativeness of the integrated sector (it contains less than 1% of the Northern Ireland pupil population) and the substantial degree of optimism about the schools' potential for solving at least part of the 'Northern Ireland problem'. Can the schools widen their base sufficiently with respect to social class and religion, to the extent that they will make a significant impact on the problem of identity? Will this involve the creation of an alternative inter-community approach which builds on the shared aspects of the two cultures?

Background

The history of education in Ireland has always been controversial whilst simultaneously providing for many people a source of optimism. In the past British administrations in Ireland attempted to proselytise Catholics through the promotion of Protestant doctrines in state-aided schools. This was an attempt to promote a form of social control which supported the other economic and cultural aspects of the British ascendancy in Ireland. By contrast, the introduction of the National Schools in 1831 was greeted at the time with some optimism by Catholic and Protestant Church authorities as an opportunity to promote more harmony and understanding between the two main religious groups in Ireland. The National System, however, became a victim of a lack of any real trust between Catholic authorities and the state on the one hand, and Catholic and Protestant educators on the other. Even the different Protestant denominations were mistrustful of each other. By the time of the disappearance of National Schools after the partition of Ireland in 1921, schools had become almost wholly denominational in ethos and administration.

The new government of Northern Ireland in 1921 also attempted to promote social cohesion when its first education minister, Lord Londonderry, proposed a non-denominational form of education for the new administration. This was in keeping with both the letter and spirit of the Government of Ireland Act which was intended to lay the foundation for equal treatment of the two traditions in Ireland. By 1930, however, ideas for reconciliation through education, had been dismantled by the two main politico-religious authorities. The Catholic

Church refused to transfer its schools to the state, whilst the Protestant Churches obtained such favourable guarantees on transfer of their schools as to render them, in effect, Protestant in philosophy and orientation.

With the significant exception of a number of integrated 'mill' schools, education since 1921 has remained denominational in character and organisation. Primary and secondary (non-grammar) schools can for all practical purposes be called either Protestant or Catholic schools. The only degree of crossover (where children attend schools of a different religious ethos and administration), of any significance, occurs within the selective grammar schools, the majority of which are still voluntary schools and not under the direction or financial control of local education authorities.

It is, however, something of a one-way process with Catholics doing almost all of the crossing-over. This can happen for a variety of reasons. The pupil might be the child of an inter-church marriage and have attended a Catholic primary school and then on transfer at 11 have gone to a Protestant voluntary grammar school. Cross-over can also be a result of geographical and demographic features where educational provision is sparse in regions where either Protestants or Catholics are only a small minority of the local school catchment. Additionally, it can be simply the selection of a better school with superior teaching or resources. Many Catholic pupils also transfer at sixteen to Protestant selective grammar schools. Although their reasons are not always clear, it appears that they are often a reaction to Northern Ireland's history of discrimination in employment. This occurs when a Catholic pupil, identified as such by employers from the school attended, is perceived to be disadvantaged in obtaining access to a range of occupations because of his or her religion. The most important area in this respect has been engineering and manufacturing occupations which have traditionally been predominantly recruited from the Protestant population. These industries are normally located in Protestant areas.

In the rest of the United Kingdom there is also some form of dual system of church schools and state schools. The significant difference in Northern Ireland is, however, that many non-Catholic parents for whatever reason, in Great Britain, send their children to Catholic primary and secondary schools. The converse is also true for Catholic parents. For the same type of schools in Northern Ireland, this degree of mixing is virtually unknown. Schools are inextricably linked to the different communities' perceptions of themselves as alternatively British/Irish/ Protestant and Irish/British/Catholic, although any definition of this complex mixture of identities will inevitably be an over-simplification.

Education and identity in Northern Ireland

Differing cultural and political identities are transmitted outwardly through subjects such as history, Irish, music and sport. Until recently, for example, that aspect of Irish history which analysed the development of republicanism in the nineteenth and twentieth century simply did not exist for most Protestant children attending Protestant schools. They were taught British history in much the same way as a pupil was in Bristol or Leeds. Such an approach was based on the hidden assumption that the history of Irish nationalism was not only irrelevant to British pupils in Northern Ireland but also potentially subversive. Cathcart (1983) analyses this feeling of ideological tunnel vision as it affected broadcasting. With respect to cultural and political identity, he argues, it was as if all references or traces of Irishness that originated outside the six counties of Northern Ireland were to be removed from the consciousness of Protestants especially, and Catholics eventually. The result of this policy was to give Protestants a diminished understanding of themselves as Irishmen and women. For Catholics, it appeared as a form of cultural assimilation and indoctrination. The two almost mutually exclusive school systems were the outward manifestation of a deeper divergence of identities between Protestants and Catholics.

Ignorance of and prejudice towards each other's beliefs and traditions is reinforced informally at school through friendships. These have a Protestant or Catholic group identity as one of their main reference points. Murray (1985) describes this as learning an alternative form of the three R's 'Religion, Ritual and Rivalry'. These include features of school life such as flags, emblems and pictures on the wall. Even among staff Murray found Protestant teachers to be more supportive of local and central educational authorities. Catholic teachers, by contrast, regarded these agencies almost as an imposition and interpreted their directives, circulars and so on with greater circumspection. Other research, however, (McEwen, 1985) has reported a substantial degree of agreement among Catholic and Protestant teachers concerning attitudes towards professional, curricular, social and political questions.

The Catholic or Protestant group identity as a determining factor of individual friendships at school has been accentuated further by the movment of the two communities since the early seventies. This is particularly so in the larger urban areas where Catholic and Protestant communities are now physically separated with the effect that opportunities for boys and girls to meet or form friendships with 'the other side' are curtailed. The voluntary division of the two groups, initially for protection from sectarian attacks, acts both as a source of security and as a powerful formative influence on attitudes to the rival community. The group ideology sets out parameters for individuals' attitudes towards members of the other denomination which are derived from a collective perception which is often based on more extreme views than those held by individuals. This can present policemen and soldiers as repressive agencies or alternatively as a courageous frontline deterrent against terrorists.

Visitors to Northern Ireland, however, are often surprised and puzzled by the apparent normality of life in the province. Apart from the presence of armed soldiers intermingling, as part of their duty, with shoppers, everyday life seems to continue without any outward sign of 'the troubles'. This is contrary to the impression which many gain from newspapers and television. The media often projects an embattled image of Northern Irish life, where normal everyday contact between people is severely limited and possible only when the shooting between the security forces and the paramilitaries stops. Darby (1986) provides a clear summary of the research findings on the continuities and discontinuities of living in Northern Ireland. He argues that there is a distinction between urban and rural communities with respect to their lack of consensus about a shared identity. Urban groups, he argues, are more polarised in this respect than Catholics or Protestants living in the country. Whilst it would be true to say that the necessities and closeness of rural life might promote more contact between Catholics and Protestants, there has nevertheless been no significant difference in the commitment to violence between urban and rural paramilitaries. The Enniskillen Remembrance Day bombing is a chilling reminder of that commitment and also an example of the way in which such an event can unite both communities in their condemnation of violence.

One of the significant factors which both groups share, Darby argues, is a sense of their regional separateness from the rest of Ireland, much in the same way that Scots, Welsh and the northern English feel distinct from other parts of Great Britain. The difference, however, in Northern Ireland is that there is insufficient common ground for the two traditions jointly to identify themselves as distinctively Northern Irish. An exception to this has been support for Northern Ireland sports teams and certain aspects of folk music. It remains true, however, that almost all aspects of life in the province tend to be refracted through the lens of sectarianism.

The absence of sufficient agreement about the nature of Northern Ireland as a separate constitutional entity is in many respects at the heart of the debate surrounding identity and imposes severe limitations on the extent of individual cross-community contacts.

Relationships between most Catholics and Protestants are conditional upon the intrusion of perceived group loyalties. As an example of this it would be difficult to hold an objective discussion between Catholics and Protestants about the role of the security forces generally in Northern Ireland and more acutely in specific cases such as the recent shooting of 'suspects' or 'terrorists' in Gibraltar. The use of alternative phrases itself is an indication of the sensitivity of the issues. This would apply to people from all walks of life, even at the level of higher education.

The voluntary principle or cultural apartheid

With such deep-seated differences between Catholic and Protestant identities the appeal of integrated education, as a means of promoting contact between the two groups, has always been strong. Opposition has equally been expressed. In particular the Catholic Church has argued that interference with the rights of the Church in respect of the 'character and identity' of Catholic schools would be the next worst thing to 'banning religion altogether' (Bishop W. Philbin, *Pastoral Letter*, Down and Connor, Easter 1975). These views represent in practice two opposing approaches to education: that it can and should be a vehicle for freedom of religious conscience. They normally complement each other since to deny freedom of conscience to a significant minority group in any democratic society will inevitably weaken the basis for social solidarity. Evidence for the former viewpoint comes from a series of public opinion polls conducted since 1967 which amongst other issues explored support for 'integrated education'. The level of agreement about its advantages has consistently been around 60% of those sampled. When parents were asked, however, if they would send their own child to such a school, the percentage of agreement dropped to approximately 30%. Although the results of polls must be interpreted with caution they nevertheless reveal a genuine feeling among many people that by attending school together Catholic and Protestant children will learn to appreciate and respect each other's values and traditions. A willingness to be pioneers in this respect seems less obvious on the part of the majority of parents. This may change rapidly as integrated schools achieve a 'critical mass' and evolve as a system of schools organically related with respect to organisation, finance and educational philosophy. At present this seems a long way in the distance.

In relation to freedom of conscience, Dunn (1986) reports that of the main religious groups in Northern Ireland, the Catholic Church has been the most strongly opposed to 'integrated education'. Such a view is consistent with Catholic theology. Loughran (1987) in a defence of Catholic education expresses it as

> The choice of a Catholic school is based on a theocratic vision of reality, which is the foundation stone of a religious system of education. It is this commitment to a fundamentally religious view of the world and of the individual which has led the Catholic Church to establish its own school system.   (Loughran, 1987)

In a Catholic school a child is taught a normal curriculum within the context of a comprehensively religious ethos. This is reflected in the organisation of the school and especially in its ethos and teaching. The imposition of an integrated educational system against the wishes of the Catholic Church would rightly be interpreted as a strike at the very heart of the principle of voluntarism in education provision. Whilst supporting such a viewpoint it could be argued that this has led to a system of cultural and educational apartheid by symbolically and administratively emphasising only the differences between Catholics and Protestants. Robinson (1971) has suggested that segregated schools have failed to diminish significantly the mistrust and suspicion between Catholics and Protestants. This, he believes, provides the seedbed for violence.

The conclusion appears to be that proponents of the voluntary principle, therefore, need to examine whether or not its promotion in Northern Ireland may be only negative in its effects in so far as segregation in schooling as the main outcome of the principle does little to lessen ignorance and prejudice within Northern Ireland.

Education and power

The practice of the voluntary principle in education by the Catholic Church has also a political dimension. Since partition in 1921, the Catholic Church has owned and staffed its own schools. It has, in effect, been the only major aspect of public life outside religion over which the Church has achieved and retained power that has been recognised and respected by successive Protestant-Unionist governments of Northern Ireland. Recent evidence of this occurred when the Department of Education for Northern Ireland set aside and almost completely ignored the findings of its own review committee on higher education, the Chilver Committee (Interim Report 1980 – Final Report 1982). This group recommended the integration of teacher education in the Greater Belfast area which would have entailed the amalgamation of St Mary's, St Joseph's (both Catholic) and Stranmillis (almost wholly Protestant with respect to student intake and staffing) Colleges of Education and the Queen's University Department of education. The two Catholic teacher education colleges were subsequently merged to form a single institution on the St Mary's site and the University Department of Education remained at its original location.

Different but equal

The position on education adopted by the Catholic Church appears to be based on the principle of equal but separate development of its schools. This concerns ideas about the nature of a Catholic identity in a state whose physical boundaries were drawn in such a way as to provide a permanent Protestant majority. In addition, the initial hopes expressed in The Government of Ireland Act (1921) of forming a bipartisan community quickly evaporated as the new state's demographic Protestant majority was translated into cultural and ideological primacies. Education was seen by the main political and religious groups as a means of securing their respective identities. Catholics saw ownership and control over their schools as a powerful means of protecting minority traditions and identity within a Protestant hegemony. Protestants, for their part, felt this equally since they perceived themselves as a potentially threatened minority in the event of a possible reunification of Ireland.

As far as the integration of schools is concerned and its potential for a shared identity, the position has been summarised concisely by Reid (1987). He argues that there are three possible perceptions about the outcomes of integration:

1. A (Protestant) + B (Catholics) = A (Assimilation of Catholics);

2. A + B = A + B (Different but equal respect for and treatment of identities);

3. A + B = C (The creation of a new agreed combined culture and identity).

At present, integrationists have not developed any clear approach to the three options above. Their rationale has been based largely on the idea that, for the moment, contact in educational and social contexts between the two communities is sufficient in itself to provide an initial conceptual rationale for the establishment and the development of existing schools. One parent interviewed by Reid crystalised the feeling of many parents when she said;

Something has happened to us all to make us choose an integrated school.

The integration movement recently received a substantial boost for its future grown with the publication of the government's educational reform proposals for Northern Ireland. These for the first time commit the DENI to the promotion of integrated schools. This contrasts sharply with the Department's earlier 'hands-off' approach when it would only fund schools when they had grown to a satisfactory size and could offer a viable curriculum. This was very much a reaction to the criticism of creating integrated schools that came from teachers' unions and the difficulties of local education authorities in rationalising a system with a significant degree of overcapacity. This has entailed closures and amalgamations of non-integrated schools with greater pupil numbers than newly created and government financed integrated schools. For the 'unions' it has meant making teachers redundant or transferring them to other schools. According to the latest government document, 'The Way Forward' (DENI, 1988), existing schools will be able to opt for 'Grant Maintained Integrated Status' on the basis of a majority of parents voting in favour of such a move. A second ballot would be held if less than half of the eligible parents voted in the first ballot, the second vote would be decisive. The government also intends to establish a central authority with the specific task of promoting integrated education within Northern Ireland.

There are presently eight planned integrated schools in Northern Ireland (two secondary and six primary) with four more at the planning stage. This represents approximately 1000, or 0.33%, of those attending primary and post-primary schools in Northern Ireland. On the surface this appears to mean that only a very small number of parents have made the decision to send their children to an integrated school. It is also the case that in some areas the demand by parents for integrated places has outstripped provision. Yet this small nucleus of schools manages to attract national and international interest and support, (including a visit by the Princess Royal), far in excess of its size or representativeness.

This can be partly explained by the way the idea of 'integrated education' projects something positive about an otherwise bleak political and ecumenical landscape. The subject uncovers questions about the deep structure of culture and ideology in Northern Ireland that have remained unresolved since partition. Attempted solutions have usually been wholly ethnocentric where one group has sought definitions with regard to identity and culture which either ignored or devalued the alternative Catholic or Protestant positions. Unfortunately violent solutions have also been attempted in part because of the absence of any middle ground. Integrated education appears to offer a more humane means of effecting social and cultural change and altering the rigidities of sectarianism.

Integrated schools are attractive to some parents because they provide an alternative educational experience with respect to their ethos and organisation. This applies specifically to the post-primary integrated schools which are comprehensive in administration and non-selective on intake at age 11. Classes, in addition, have been organised along mixed-ability lines. Such educational policies contrast sharply with most other schools in Northern Ireland which are still overwhelmingly selective with the 11+ 'test' continuing to exercise a baneful effect on the primary curriculum. Primary schools are often forced through parental pressure to concentrate single-mindedly on achieving as many 'passes' as possible. This necessarily restricts the width of the primary experience for some children. It also does little for the confidence of those children (73%) who are often perceived as 'failures' at eleven. It means also that the secondary (non-grammar) schools have to recapture and restore the confidence of many of their eleven year-old pupils who are crudely labelled as 'non-academic' or non-grammar school material.

The schools' adoption of egalitarian policies with regard to intake and the absence of streaming also challenges Northern Ireland's predominantly selective system which adds another of ostensibly academic segregation to the existing denominational separation of children. Successive reports from the Northern Ireland Council for Educational Research (NICER) have also shown that, similar to Great Britain in the fifties and sixties, selection at 11+ appears to have an inbuilt social class bias and disadvantages children from manual-working backgrounds. They also show that too many children from manual backgrounds achieve less than their potential even when they gain a scholarship to a selective school (Sutherland and Gallagher, 1986; Wilson, 1985). The non-selective nature of the post-primary integrated schools, therefore, offers for many parents a means of avoiding the academic pressure of, for example, excessive coaching at school or by visiting the homes of 'freelance' teachers who specialise in coaching. In addition, choosing an integrated school also relieves much of the emotional strain associated with the 11+ test.

Conclusion

This chapter has set out the background to the present denominational arrangements in Northern Ireland's educational system. This has involved essentially a struggle over identity between originally the colonial power (Britain) and chiefly the local Irish Catholic population. Latterly, this struggle has been continued in Northern Ireland after partition in 1921, between the majority Protestant and minority Catholic communities. This has resulted in two separate educational sub-systems, one state administered but effectively Protestant in ethos and administration, and the other Catholic in ownership and practice. Unlike Great Britian, where similar denominational arrangements exist, there is no significant cross-over of pupils between the two systems.

Despite the present 'troubles', from 1969 onwards, the two systems have evolved long-established points of contact. One of these, for example, concerns the interests of the selective grammar schools which are furthered by the Governing Bodies Association on which Catholics and Protestants are both represented. With respect to the primary and secondary (non-grammar) schools, relationships are largely infrequent and informal through, for example, sport and school organised holidays. Since the outbreak of disorder in 1969, however, many people in Northern Ireland have asked whether or not contacts should be made more formal even to the extent of educating Catholic and Protestant children together in order to promote political and social consensus. This is to place education at the forefront of creating social cohesion, against a discouraging background in Northern Ireland of economic discrimination and cultural disadvantage of Catholics. Catholic school leavers, for example, are still twice as likely to be unemployed as their Protestant counterparts. Research evidence on the ability of schools to deliver social and economic reforms is at best inconclusive and at worst discouraging. Rutter (1979) is slightly more optimistic but Jencks (1973) in the USA and Halsey (1980) in the UK are largely pessimistic about using education as a vehicle for wider social reforms. Halsey sees little evidence that post-war egalitarian policies and re-organisation, through comprehensivisation after 1965 in England and Wales, have achieved little by way of altering disparities of educational opportunity in the face of social class divisions.

Other contributors to this debate argue that education is overwhelmingly conservative in relation to existing social, political and economic hierarchies (Bowles and Gintis, 1976; Miliband, 1968). Within the context of these last two approaches the segregated system in Northern Ireland is consequent upon a larger struggle between the two communities about such issues as the distribution of jobs, the best farming land and political power. The fact that maths and science subjects are studied to a greater extent by Protestants (McEwen and Curry, 1986); (Osborne, 1985) provides some evidence that these economically important subjects have been claimed by the Protestant community as part of its intellectual and economic 'property' (Bernstein, 1971). This has been reflected in the absence of any significant degree of access by Catholics to the main employers of skilled technical, scientific and manufacturing labour. The imbalance has also been caused through the physical 'ownership' of such work by its location in predominantly Protestant districts.

The main conclusion that can be drawn from this debate is that educational reforms by themselves will not deliver the foundation for social cohesion in Northern Ireland (Salters, 1970). If harmony is to be achieved in the long run economic and cultural reforms are also required. There are encouraging signs that the government is prepared to do this by replacing the present employment watchdog, The Fair Employment Agency, with a new strengthened body. Proponents of integrated education see it also as a much needed reform not only in breaking the selective mould of Northern Ireland schools, but also in the promotion of Catholic and Protestant cultures and identities as partners of equal worth. Whether or not this leads to some new form of identity is unclear and unlikely against the background of the deep historical divisions which exist between the two sections of Irish society. Sceptics might argue that at best integrated schools can only appeal to a small section of both communities with similar and largely middle-class backgrounds and aspirations. It might also be attractive to a small limited group of Catholic and Protestant parents who want their children educated in schools free from any direct association with any of the main churches.

Since 1981, when the first planned integrated school was founded, there has been a substantial growth of the sector. In addition the integrated movement has succeeded in convincing the government to put its weight behind the development of new schools by placing a statutory duty on its department of education to promote religiously integrated education. This, by any standards, has been a significant achievement although not without considerable cost to some communities and effort by the teaching staff (see Chapter 6). It is not without its problems, however, not least of which is the choice and execution of a strategy for the majority of segregated schools that will adapt existing and promote new projects of inter-community understanding and respect. This is presently being attempted through government sponsored programmes such as 'Education for Mutual Understanding'. This gives financial and other encouragements for Catholic and Protestant schools to develop inter-school activities involving, for example, joint local history studies or shared school educational visits. At first sight, this seems to contradict the government's policy of encouraging understanding through the development of the integrated sector. It remains to be seen whether or not these two strategies are complementary with the integrated sector providing a bridge between what are always going to be the two main education systems.

Chapter 12

Curriculum in Small Primary Schools

Leslie Caul
(Lecturer, Stranmillis College, Belfast)

Introduction

There are 985 primary schools in Northern Ireland with enrolments ranging from 5 to 1144 pupils. While the mean enrolment in primary schools is 185 pupils, it is more likely that schools will have many fewer pupils on their rolls than 185 children (median enrolment 124 pupils). In fact, 43% of primary schools have enrolments of less than 100 pupils. Schools with enrolments of between 50-200 pupils represent 46% of the total number of all primary schools. Only 47 schools (5%) have enrolments of over 500 pupils. Of the total number of primary schools in the province 635 (64%) have a teaching principal. These schools serve 54 368 pupils, 30% of the school population. This chapter looks at small primary schools with teaching principals such as that described by Emma Caul in Chapter 8 and asks: Are such schools deficient in that they fail to provide a sufficiently rich curriculum for their pupils?

Since 1978 the future of the small primary school in Northern Ireland has become increasingly uncertain. Demographic trends coupled with a government demand for accountability and value for money in the provision of public services has led to the implementation of a policy of rationalisation.

A substantial body of opinion has developed among administrators that, by virtue of their size, small primary schools are inherently disadvantaged both educationally and socially and thus there are sound reasons, besides financial considerations, that schools below a minimum pupil size should be closed. Such a policy was articulated by the Department of Education for Northern Ireland in 1983.

Among the criticisms of small primary schools three features emerge as significant. Firstly, it is argued that by virtue of size small schools cannot provide adequately sized peer groups for their children, who consequently suffer socially. Secondly, that the location of small primary schools and the limited size of their teaching staff create conditions of teacher isolation and thirdly, as Bell and Sigsworth (1987) suggest, the major criticism is that small schools cannot provide a curriculum of adequate breadth and balance. This chapter considers the latter assertion and reviews curricular provision in small primary schools in Northern Ireland and in Scotland. The chapter considers the age, experience and qualifications of teachers in small primary schools, the facilities available at the school, the aims of education in such schools and the range of curricular provision in each location.

Education in the small school

Both the Plowden and Gittins Reports (1967) devoted particular attention to small primary schools. The two reports were opposed to pupil classification by streaming for example:

> We welcome unstreaming in the infant or first school and hope that it will continue to spread through the age groups of the junior and middle schools.   (Plowden para. 819)

The Gittins Report did not rule out homogeneous groups but argued against the tendency for ability groups to become rigid and rejected any possibility that a small school's inability to arrange its class in ability groups could be considered a defect.

The reports paid tribute to the work of teachers in small schools:

> Acknowledgement must be made of the devoted work of many village school teachers. Often working along with few opportunities for discussion with their colleagues, sometimes heavily handicapped by their buildings, responsible for children of a wider age range than most junior teachers think practicable, they have created schools characterised by warmth, forbearance and an almost family affect.   (Plowden, para. 77)

Both committees commented unfavourably on the generally poor state of small school buildings, especially when compared with the often superior standard of urban school provision. Allied to this both reports questioned the economics of small primary schools in terms of cost effectiveness. Indeed Gittins identified the higher costs, measured in unit-costs per pupil, of provision in an area of low population density mainly as a result of higher pupil-teacher ratios:

> Where there is a large number of small schools needing very gen-

erous staffing, education is likely to be more expensive than in a compact area with a small number of large schools.

(Gittins, para. 5.7.8)

It was argued, however, that there was no evidence to show that greater expenditure resulted in better education or that small schools were inferior. Plowden rejected any notion that small schools' attainment measures differed from those in larger urban situations.

It was on the question of the curriculum provided by primary schools that both Plowden and Gittins directed their main concerns about the small school. These concerns were not evident in the Hadow Report (1931) or the even earlier *Handbook of Suggestions* (1905). However, by the 1960s a new definition of an appropriate primary school curriculum had appeared and what had once been considered adequate had become deficient:

> The curriculum of the primary school is now much wider and richer than when many primary schools were first built. The goals proposed by modern primary education challenge the limited space and resources of the small school . . . some aspects of the curriculum, such as drama, physical education and expressive movement and science tend to be weak . . . the opportunity for this kind of co-operation (use of specialist skills) is limited in a small school.

(Gittins, para. 7.5.6)

Both committees regarded small primary schools as under-resourced and as incapable of fostering the evolving emphasis on pupil interaction since the small size of peer groups restricted the potential of group work. However, the small number of teachers and an assumption that this necessarily implied a limited curriculum caused the greatest concern. Plowden recommended that 'schools with an age range of 5–11 should usually have at least three classes each covering two age groups'.

Gittins recommended that the minimum size of a school be fifty to sixty pupils and three teachers. However, the Committee also argued strongly for a centrallly located area school with a minimum of six teachers.

The curriculum of the small primary school

Open any inspector's report on an individual school and you are unlikely, so far as it comments upon curriculum quality, to have much idea of its size. This conclusion is supported by the periodic reviews produced by HMI's who summarise the major themes to have emerged from individual inspectors. Those issued to date contain little indication that the size of primary schools is related to the quality of their curricula. A study of the breadth of the curricula in rural schools carried out at Aston University (1981) found little evidence to substantiate the view that the curricula were restricted:

> The fears often expressed about the limited curriculum of small schools received very little support from the visits, except in the case of science, which is a weakness in primary education by no means restricted to small schools. Music, one of the two subjects generally considered difficult to provide for, had good provision in all the schools . . . physical education, the other subject area most often regarded as difficult to provide for, was not seriously restricted.

(The Social Effects of Rural Primary School Re-organisation, Final Report, p. 34)

The HMI report on Norfolk (HMI, 1984) expressed the view that the curriculum in small primary schools was likely to be restricted although there was considerable variation between schools:

> Over a third of the (primary) schools in the survey had fewer than sixty pupils on roll. It is difficult for such small schools with only two or three staff and limited resources, to provide a curriculum of breadth and intellectual stimulation but to their great credit some were managing to do so.

(Educational Provision and Response in some Norfolk Schools, para. 39)

However a report by the Scottish Education Department in 1974 on primary schools in Inverness-shire provides a different conclusion.

> Pupils are lively, responsive, knowledgeable and industrious and join, regardless of age, in art and craft activities, outdoor expeditions and discussing and writing about subjects of common interest, all without detriment to progress in basic skills. There is no doubt that the atmosphere of intimacy among staff, pupils and parents which exists in the one to four teacher schools is a contributing factor in the success of those which have adopted these desirable approaches to primary education.

(Education in Inverness-shire p. 22)

In a follow up to ORACLE Galton *et al* investigated the breadth of curriculum in small schools and although no results have been published to date Galton has indicated that substantial variations were found between the nine local authorities from which the sample of schools were drawn. In the study there were few differences of any significance between large and small schools. An OECD/CERI survey of rural educational provision in developed countries does not lend much credence to the view that achievement is associated with size of school. Sher (1981) comments:

> There are bits and pieces of evidence that students in rural schools do as well or even slightly better than urban students on basic literacy and mathematical tests. Other reports give the impression that rural student attainment is below average.
>
> (Rural Education in Urbanised Nations, p. 50)

Studies of the quality of curricular provision in small schools indicate that there are enormous differences. Bell and Sigsworth (1987) argue that some of the best and some of the worst primary education is probably to be found in small schools. This is the view that Gittins took and leaves the case against small schools at a level of supposition and apparent logic.

Contemporary thinking regarding primary school education highlights recent concerns about deficiencies in the primary curriculum. Bolton (1985) summarises the problem of balance in the primary curriculum as follows:

> The key question relating to these curricular issues raised by Primary Education in England is that of how to make the best use of the curricular strengths of all the teachers. Essentially this question is about the balance between class teaching and the use of specialists in some form or other.　　　(Curriculum, 5–16 pp. 199–215)

The question is not about having a minimum number of teachers in a school but about how a means can be found to use the skills and knowledge of the whole staff to improve the curriculum throughout the school.

In Northern Ireland a set of written guidelines published by the Northern Ireland Council for Educational Development attempt to provide a framework for curriculum development. The guidelines adopt a theory-practice perspective and by incorporating a school-based curriculum review attempt to stimulate a school-wide discussion of relevant approaches to working with children. It is within this context of curriculum development that Bell and Sigsworth (1987) suggest that there is a structured weakness in small schools when measured against a national framework. In particular small schools appear to lack an adequate number of teachers to stimulate debate about curricular issues.

The 'disciplinary' emphasis contained in the individual curricular guidelines provide a clear indication that it is intended that specialist teaching should be introduced to the primary school. Campbell (1985) shows that 'some of the major educational documents have transmitted a gradually clarifying image of the responsibility and significance of the curriculum postholder'. This view was echoed in *Primary Education* (1974):

> The teacher with such knowledge (specialism) would still have general responsibility for a group of children but she would also advise on the teaching of her special subject and be available for consultation; in this way the whole school would benefit.
>
> (*Primary Education*, p. 15)

Campbell's work demonstrates the existence of problems inherent to the demands being made on post holders to sustain curriculum development. This role requires a range of complex interpersonal skills without which the most knowledgeable specialist is likely to be ineffectual beyond her own classroom. Campbell argues:

> (These skills) in addition to demanding considerable charm and character, also required sensitivity and tact, and a number of head-teachers made the point that such personal qualities in the post holders were pre-requisites for the successful implementation of the development.   (Campbell, 1985, p. 53)

Small schools, however, are seen to be structurally incapable of having a specialist staff who can cover a full range of the curricular areas and are prone to suffer an inadequate and restricted curriculum. Yet their size, number of teachers and sometimes architectural peculiarities can lend themselves more easily to professional openness and exchange of ideas which collegiality (Hoyle, 1974) demands. However, an official literature does suggest this:

> Because of our notions of stereotypical rural residents, we often assume the urban model to be the preferred model to which all people aspire.   (Darnell, 1981, p. 34)

There are a number of advantages that can be claimed for the small school. Foremost among the claims are what King (1978) calls a 'family atmosphere'. As the Schools Council report:

By far the most significant advantage of the small school from the point of view of the child was the close relationship between pupil and teacher.   (Schools Council, 1975, p. 5)

Besides the ease of establishing a family atmosphere, a further advantage is the task of ensuring curriculum continuity. As Bell and Sigsworth (1987) argue:

It is as if the characteristics of traditional small scale communities of people dealing with each other, not so much as occupants of particular roles, but as people personally well known to each other infuses the school also.   (Bell and Sigsworth, 1987, p. 158)

The comparative ease with which small schools are able to form close links with parents is also one of their potentially advantageous characteristics. Again the Schools Council noted in their 1975 report:

Nearly all teachers spoke of the easy and friendly relationships which a small school staff were able to establish with parents.
(Schools Council, p. 64)

The considerable flexibility that enables a teacher to organise the curriculum in a variety of ways is seen by Bell and Sigsworth as a strength. This enables teachers to focus on one or more aspects of the curriculum at any one time and facilitates a curriculum which is less marked by subject division.

Plowden's view that 'pupils do not see the world in separate subjects is one that is relevant to the small school'.

An inevitable feature of small primary schools is that classes contain children whose ages span more than one year. The Inspectorate in the 1974 Teachers' Guide suggested that considerable care is necessary in composite classes to match the level of difficulty of work set to the pupil's capabilities. However, Bennett *et al.* (1987) found no significant difference between teachers of single-age or mixed-age classes in their ability to set work of appropriate levels of difficulty. Bell and Sigsworth (1987) see the age mix, together with the children's extended time with the same class teacher, as a positive incentive to devise a more individually differentiated curriculum in which pupils spend more of their time working independently. There is evidence that small schools do have some success in developing a greater sense of independence in their pupils. The Aston University study suggested that:

Having been accustomed to working for much of their time on their own, they (pupils of small schools) could be given more responsibility for the organisation of their school work.

(The Social Effects of Rural Primary School Re-organisation Final Report 1981, p. 35)

Although it would appear that the available evidence does not suggest that the case against the small school is in any way conclusive the argument that they offer an educational experience which is in some way deficient is often repeated. The familiarity of the arguments of limitations of size and restricted curriculum has often made the rationalisation process easier. However, new interest in what happens in small primary schools is re-opening the debate and attempting to support the arguments presented with evidence. The main issues of concern are subject specialism and the socialisation process. Both are potential strengths and weaknesses in all schools.

Research into small primary schools

The debates about closing small primary schools have led to feelings of vulnerability on the part of those who teach in small schools and this has led to the myth that small school research must be difficult. It is undoubtedly a sensitive issue and all research in this area must have a concern for those who teach and those who learn in our small schools. This chapter is based on an attempt to obtain information which would inform the small school debate within the context of such concern.

Two local authorities, one in Northern Ireland and one in Scotland, were approached to seek permission to use schools with a teaching principal in their area for the research. Schools considered appropriate by the local authorities were identified and complete confidentiality of information from individual schools was assured. A covering letter and questionnaire was sent to each of the participating schools in March 1987. The letter explained the purpose of the research and sought the co-operation of the principal in completing the questionnaire. The confidentiality of the information was stressed and the name and location of the school was not required unless the principal was willing to be a participant in any follow-up research.

The questionnaire was designed to obtain detailed information about the school in six different areas and allowed additional comment in a seventh section:

1. The teaching staff
2. The school's resources and organisation
3. The aims of the school
4. The curriculum offered to pupils

5. The teaching methods used
6. School-home relationships
7. Additional comment and individual response.

Characteristics of teaching stock

The research was designed to look specifically at schools with four or fewer teachers. This group of schools represents 43% of the total number of schools in Northern Ireland. The Northern Ireland sample had between two and four full-time teachers, there were no single-teacher schools. The range in the Scottish schools was, however, between one and four. The mean for both samples was 2.5 (Table 12.1).

In both samples there were significantly more full-time female teachers than male and where part-time teachers were a regular feature of the teaching force they were always females. The Scottish schools used proportionately more part-time staff but the Northern Ireland schools used their part-time teachers for a greater number of hours per week (Table 12.1).

The age structure of the principal teachers in both the Northern Ireland Irish and Scottish samples shows a marked similarity as does their overall teaching experience. However the principals in the Northern Ireland schools have spent significantly longer in their present post. The mean of 12.2 years as principal of a small school demonstrates considerable stability of service in the sample (see Table 12.2). Since the greater proportion of female to male teachers in the small school has already been shown (Table 12.1) it is not surprising that there are

Table 12.1   *Teachers by Number, Gender and Part-time Provision*

	Northern Ireland Schools	Scottish Schools
Full-time Teachers	2.45	2.45
	(2–4)	(1–4)
Female Full-time Teachers	2.00	1.80
	(1–3)	(1–3)
Male Full-time Teachers	0.40	0.60
	(0–1)	(0–1)
Part-time Teachers	0.50	1.82
Part-time Hours	5.3	3.8

Table 12.2   Age, Teaching Experience and Sex of Principal Teachers

	Principal Northern Ireland		Principal Scotland	
Mean Age	43.8	yrs	42.2	yrs
Minimum Age	30	yrs	28	yrs
Maximum Age	58	yrs	57	yrs
Mean Teaching Experience in Present School	12.2	yrs	8.3	yrs
Minimum Experience	1	yr	1	yr
Maximum Experience	32	yrs	17	yrs
Mean Overall Teaching Experience	19.9	yrs	18.7	yrs
Male Principals	8		5	
Female Principals	14		6	

predominantly more female principals although the proportion is significantly smaller than that in the total sample.

The data obtained from the principal teachers on their qualifications shows that more of the Northern Ireland sample had teaching certificates which are usually awarded on the completion of teacher training while the Scottish principals were more likely to have had a university based training. However the numbers, particularly in the Scottish sample, are rather small for conclusions to be drawn from this. Table 12.3 gives the distribution of qualifications of the principal teachers in both Northern Ireland and Scotland.

Enrolments in schools

The questionnaire was designed to obtain data on the enrolments of the small schools in the study in a number of years 1974–75, 1979–80, 1985–86 and 1986–87. It is interesting to note that the means for the first and second specified years actually show an increase in pupil enrolment in both Northern Ireland and Scotland (see Table 12.4). However since 1980 the Scottish schools average enrolment has shown a dramatic decline of some ten pupils. In Northern Ireland there was some decline between 1980 and 1986 but the last two years have indicated stability in numbers.

Table 12.3 The Qualifications of Principal Teachers

Qualification	Northern Ireland	Scotland
Certificate	72%	45%
	(16)	(5)
Diploma	36%	36%
	(8)	(4)
B.Ed.	9%	9%
	(2)	(1)
B.A.	22%	18%
	(5)	(2)
B.Sc.	9%	9%
	(2)	(1)
M.A.	5%	18%
	(1)	(2)

Curricular aims: developmental

The principals were asked to rank order a set of developmental aims of the curriculum. These were reflected in the following aspects of development – aesthetic, emotional, intellectual, moral, physical, social and spiritual. The teachers in the Northern Ireland sample, with the exception of one, ranked intellectual development as either 1 or 2, thus this aspect of development would seem to be the primary aim of the curriculum in these small schools (see Figure 1). Less than half of the principals in Scotland indicated a first preference for intellectual development but if the score was not high it tended to be of a low order in the rankings. With such unanimity in regard to intellectual development, the other developmental aims were less clearly defined in the Northern Ireland sample. In the Scottish sample a higher value was placed on a number of developmental aims than in Northern Ireland. Principals in Scotland saw emotional development as very important (see Figure 2). However social development was clearly the first preference in Scottish schools.

In Scotland social and emotional aims were ranked highly with over two-thirds of the sample ranking these aims first or second. Social development was most often ranked third or fourth in Northern Ireland (more than 50% of the sample) while in Scotland 67% ranked this aim first or second. The Scottish sample ranked emotional development at number one frequently but if you take the first three rankings together

Table 12.4   Mean Enrolments in Schools 1974–87

Enrolments Mean Number	N.I.	Scotland
1975	55.1	49
	(11–95)	(24–100)
1980	56.8	53.3
	(11–149)	(21–111)
1986	53	52.2
	(9–104)	(23–113)
1987	53.5	42.7
	(18–108)	(12–86)

both samples appear to regard emotional development as having considerable importance – Northern Ireland 64% and Scotland 73% (see Table 12.5).

While aesthetic development, physical and spiritual development were not ranked highly by either sample there was considerable variability in how they were viewed. In Northern Ireland aesthetic development

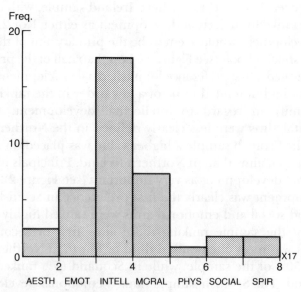

Figure 1   Developmental Aims (NI)

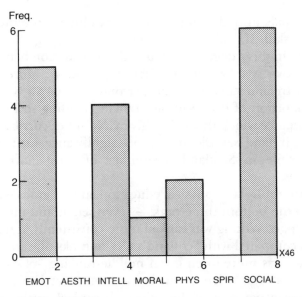

Figure 2   Developmental Aims (SCOT)

was most frequently ranked seventh (45%) while in Scotland spiritual development was most often in that position (77%).

Physical development was either ranked highly at number one (44%) or much lower at number six (27%) in Scotland while in Northern Ireland it was much more frequently given a middle ranking – almost 60% ranked it three, four or five.

Table 12.5   Percentage Rank Order of Developmental Curricular Aims

| | Ranks 1 & 2 | | Ranks 6 & 7 | |
	N.I.	Scotland	N.I.	Scotland
Aesthetic	15.0	0	45.0	22.0
Emotional	30.0	54.0	15.0	11.0
Intellectual	90.0	44.0	0	11.0
Moral	40.0	11.0	35.0	11.0
Physical	5.0	22.0	30.0	44.0
Social	10.0	67.0	25.0	22.0
Spiritual	10.0	0	50.0	78.0

Curricula aims: skills

The principals in both samples regard reading as the most important curricular skill. If ranks one and two are taken together 82% of both groups fall in this category, although the distribution between rank one and rank two is different (see Figures 3 and 4). More principals in Northern Ireland rank it as number one (73%-64%). Nevertheless the large proportion of both samples ranking reading so highly indicates the importance which this skill is given. No other curricular skill in the Northern Ireland sample shows any significance in its number one ranking while in Scotland a number of areas have very similar frequencies.

In Northern Ireland physical education and religious education were ranked in the bottom three ranks – seven, eight and nine – by 68% of the principals. Writing was ranked more consistently at three, four and five, 82% compared with Scotland's 65% at ranks one and two. General knowledge was more often given middle ranking – 45% at ranks four and five – as was science which was ranked at five or six by 50%. Seventy-seven per cent of the principals ranked maths as one or two suggesting that these skills with those of reading are the most important elements in the curriculum of Northern Ireland schools (see Table 12.6).

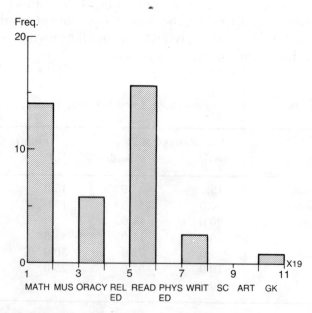

Figure 3   Curricular Aims (NI)

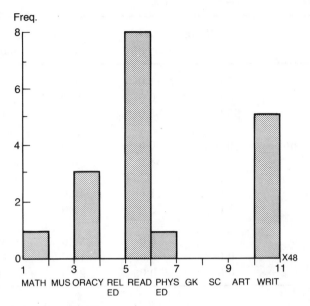

Figure 4   Curricular Aims (SCOT)

In Scotland after reading and writing there appears to be greater variation in the importance given to various curricular areas than in Northern Ireland. Mathematics, in particular, is not as significant but rather takes its place with physical and religious education, general knowledge and science.

Curricular aims: personal

Principals in both Northern Ireland and Scotland ranked 'enjoyment of school' as the single most important personal aim for their pupils. It was ranked number one by 55% of Scottish principals and as one or two by 65% of the principals in Northern Ireland. Beyond that agreement there was considerable diversity within and between samples (see Table 12.7). The ability to make reasoned judgements was important to both sets of principals with over 40% of them giving it top ranking. Obedience and criticism were identified in the Scottish sample as important aims but in the Northern Ireland sample adaptability, reasoned judgements and individualism were the next most important aims although of considerably less importance.

Obedience and self control were not consistently ranked highly and inventiveness and critical ability were ranked by more than two-thirds of the Northern Ireland principals no higher than five.

Table 12.6   *Percentage Rank Order of Skills Aims*

| | Ranks 1 & 2 | | Ranks 8–10 | |
	N.I.	Scotland	N.I.	Scotland
Maths	70.0	11.0	0.0	0.0
Music	0.0	0.0	25.0	44.0
Oracy	30.0	33.0	25.0	11.0
Religious Education	0.0	0.0	45.0	55.0
Reading	80.0	88.0	0.0	11.0
Physical Education	0.0	11.0	40.0	22.0
Writing	15.0	55.0	0.0	11.0
General Knowledge	5.0	0.0	30.0	33.0
Science	0.0	0.0	10.0	11.0
Art	0.0	0.0	25.0	0.0

Table 12.7   *Percentage Rank Order of Personal Aims*

| | Ranks 1 &2 | | Ranks 8–10 | |
	N.I.	Scotland	N.I.	Scotland
Enjoyment of School	65.0	55.0	10.0	0.0
Adaptability	30.0	0.0	10.0	22.0
Reasoned judgements	45.0	33.0	10.0	33.0
Criticism	5.0	44.0	75.0	44.0
Obedience	20.0	33.0	35.0	78.0
Self control	0.0	11.0	0.0	11.0
Individualism	25.0	11.0	25.0	0.0
Inventiveness	10.0	11.0	35.0	11.0

While the principals appeared to consider individuality important or at least to merit middle rankings those aspects of development most closely associated with the individual's capacity to be individual, i.e. his inventiveness and his ability to be critical appear to be regarded as relatively unimportant. In both samples the ability to make reasoned judgements appears considerably less important (see Figures 5 and 6).

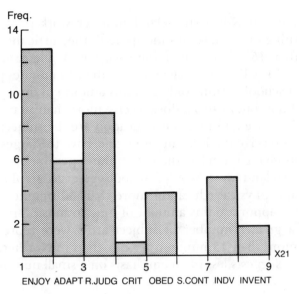

Figure 5   *Personal Aims (NI)*

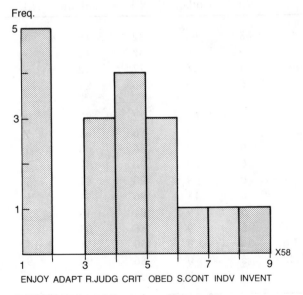

Figure6   *Personal Aims (SCOT)*

Curriculum

In small schools in Northern Ireland number work (77%), reading (68%) and writing (59%) make up the spine of the curriculum and are given more than 15 minutes attention each day. While reading (54%) and number work (64%) are also given more than 15 minutes per day in many Scottish schools writing only gets this amount of time per day in 36% of the schools but in 46% it does receive more than 30 minutes per week. Poetry, science and religious education are the subjects in both samples which receive the least attention and have the largest proportion of schools giving them less than 30 minutes per week (Table 12.8). In Northern Ireland over 80% of schools give geography, history, needlework and physical education more than 30 minutes per week while over 90% apportion this amount of time to music, art and craft. In Scotland a greater number of subject areas were represented as being given more than 15 minutes per day than in Northern Ireland which perhaps suggests less of an emphasis on a small number of core subjects.

Table 12.8   Subjects by Time Spent in Small Schools (in percentages)

Subjects	15 mins per day		More than 30 mins per week		Less than 30 mins per week	
	N.I.	Scotland	N.I.	Scotland	N.I.	Scotland
Reading	68	63	32	18	0	9
Writing	59	36	32	45	5	9
Composition	14	18	77	72	5	9
Poetry	5	9	55	27	41	54
Number work	77	63	22	27	0	9
Geography	9	9	86	63	5	9
History	9	9	86	63	5	9
Music	0	0	96	82	5	9
Art	0	9	96	81	5	9
Craft	0	18	96	54	5	18
Science	5	9	64	46	32	27
Needdlework	5	9	86	63	9	9
Religious Ed.	36	9	50	54	14	27
Physical Ed.	5	0	86	90	9	0
Others	9	9	27	36	4	0

Conclusion

The information displayed in this chapter ranges from the sex and age of principals and teachers, through the facilities of the school, the organisation of schools and classes to the aims of the school and the time spent on various aspects of the curriculum. In terms of policy regarding small schools the evidence in the Scottish sample of greater peripatetic support might suggest a greater level of commitment to sustaining small schools. However, although there were fewer part-time teachers in Northern Ireland they did work for a longer period of time.

There is evidence in the Scottish sample of more integration and greater flexibility in the curriculum. Schools in both areas appeared to give time to areas of the curriculum which, it is claimed, are neglected in small schools, i.e. music, craft, needlework and physical education. Schools in Scotland benefit from a more supportive policy in providing for these aspects of schooling. The open statements of the principals in Northern Ireland seem to reflect such a feeling of isolation and lack of support. There appears to be a belief that school policy is devised with the best interest of large schools uppermost and that the small schools adapt as they may. However, they also express the advantages of the small school at every level from the individual attention given to the pupils to the coherence of the curriculum.

This chapter has provided information on the aims and curriculum of the small school set in the context of the physical and academic resources provided. There are some indications that not all of the myths about small schools are true and that the advantages may not all be on the social and personal side at the expense of the educational and purely academic. In particular the chapter provides information about the perceptions of teachers of the job they do and the curriculum offered to the pupils and relates clearly to the earlier perceptions of Emma Caul in Chapter 8. The numbers in the samples analysed were small and given the form of the research the results obtained could be distorted by a single rogue response. However, the interest and effort of the teachers in the completion of the questionnaire would seem to suggest a high level of commitment to their schools and their pupils. The numbers in these samples need to be enlarged and a comparison drawn with a number of large schools. The differences suggested between Scotland and Northern Ireland in terms of policy and implementation need further investigation. It would also be both interesting and valuable to include schools in England, Wales and the Republic of Ireland so that a view of the aims and the curriculum of small schools throughout the British Isles could be formed.

The advent of a National Curriculum would seem to add impetus to the need for such a study to be carried out as soon as possible. This would then provide a baseline for a review of the effects of a National Curriculum on what happens in schools at some time in the future.

Chapter 13

Policy Implications of a Study of Persistent Absentees

Joan Harbison
(Lecturer, Stranmillis College, Belfast)

Introduction

There has been an apparent failure in Northern Ireland's schools to meet the needs of many pupils. This is especially true in and around Belfast where a high concentration of disaffected youth resides in the west of the city. In 1985 around 30% of children left school without any form of certification. Indeed, this failure is exacerbated by a continual concentration of persistent absenteeism in the 15–16 year-old age range. This has been highlighted by a survey of attendance carried out by the Central Economic Service of the Department of Finance (1977). In 1977, 7.8% (26 500 pupils) of compulsory school age missed more than 15% of possible school days. By 1982 the proportion had fallen to 6.1% (19 147 pupils). This decrease was most evident in the group of children who were classified as absent for reasons other than illness. The group classified as unjustifiably absent decreased from 4.2% (14 255 pupils) to 2% (6 153 pupils). However, of this smaller proportion a greater number (68.4%) were found to be absent with the knowledge of their parents who in many cases gave consent for non-attendance at school. These 'condoned absentees' were most prevalent in the 15–16 year-old age range. Nevertheless the dramatic decrease within the group of pupils who were judged absent for reasons other than physical illness must have been influenced by some action on the part of the school since there was no apparent change in the personal, social and family characteristics of the group. The disadvantaged nature of the group is evident from the analysis of the socio-economic data collected. The characteristics evident in the literature from Tyerman (1968) to Galloway (1985) of pupils who often needed help in school, who had sometimes been before the courts and who were more likely to come from one-parent families, above-average size families who were in receipt of some form of social security, were still there. Knowing the characteristics of pupils who are judged to be absent for reasons other than illness, i.e. their absence is unjustified, does not explain why they are absent nor what can be done about it. There is also no available explanation for the increasing tendency towards non-attendance as the pupils grow older. The problem is exacerbated in areas of high-density population as the prevalence of the associated socio-economic conditions are greater there and the numbers involved are by definition larger.

In 1985 the Department of Education initiated a pilot study to learn more about this group of 'condoned' absentees not just from surveys, school records, educational welfare officers or teachers but from the pupils themselves and from their parents. If what we do to and for pupils in school is a variable in attendance and is to be incorporated within any explanation of pupil absence then it becomes necessary not only to accept the pupil's view as legitimate but also to accept the assumption that pupils react positively to a favourable school ethos (they attend) and negatively to what they perceive as irrelevant curricula (they don't attend). In such a model the pupil is seen as a consumer making a rational choice in respect of the product on offer. However only very recently has research such as that of Reid (1985) and Galloway (1985) taken the pupil's perceptions into account. Reid on the basis of 120 semi-structured interviews with pupils painted a picture of low achievers, disenchanted with teachers, the curriculum and school life, who largely blamed the institution for their absence. Galloway's picture focused on stress factors in the pupils' lives including overcrowding, unemployment, poverty and chronic illness and concluded that the pupils' absence represented a legitimate and rational response to these circumstances – school had become largely peripheral to their lives. The study initiated by the Department of Education attempted to examine both the views of the consumers, parents and pupils about school and their perception of non-attendance.

Study

Since the evidence exists for expecting non-attendance to be more prevalent in urban areas and in the fourth and fifth year of secondary education the sample was drawn from eight Belfast secondary schools. Four were from the maintained school sector, i.e. administered by the Maintained Schools Commission of the Roman Catholic Church and four were controlled schools administered by the Belfast Education and Library Board for the Department of Education (N.I.). Three were single-sex female, three single-sex male and two were co-educational.

Two schools each from the north, south, east and west of the city were selected.

A total of 293 fourth and fifth year pupils were found to have been absent for a period in excess of fourteen days during the term September-December 1985. (Figures for absence due to illness were unavailable for two of the schools.) Of these pupils 122 from 119 families were identified as having been absent for reasons other than illness or where illness explained less than 50% of the absence (Table 13.1).

The selection of the sample to be interviewed was not random but determined by the prevalent classifications of the education welfare officer in a particular school. Where the pupil's absence was identified as for 'no apparent reason and with parents' knowledge', i.e. condoned absence then the selection of the pupils for interview was straightforward.

However some education welfare officers identified few, if any, absences in this way and so pupils falling in the 'mixed' or 'other reasons' (and this included suspension), categories were used as the basis of selection. In eight cases the education welfare officer or the teacher who completed the questionnaire indicated that family circumstances would make it inappropriate to approach that family (Table 13.2).

Eighty one parents in all were contacted by letter. Seven indicated that they were unable to take part because of family difficulties, eleven declined to be included and in nine cases it proved impossible to gain entry. Fifty-four interviews with parents were completed (Table 13.2).

One parent declined to have his child included in the survey, four pupils left at Easter and were not available for interview and fourteen pupils were unavailable due to absence from school. Thirty-eight pupil interviews were completed (Table 13.3).

Methodology

Using an amended form of the 1982 survey questionnaire which reduced the nine categories of absence to six, education welfare officers and teachers were asked to classify the absence of the pupils in the fourth and fifth year of the schools included who had been absent in excess of fourteen days between September and Christmas 1985. The categories were:

1) More than 50% of the absence due to illness;
2) Pupil was absent without parents' knowledge;
3) Pupil was absent with parents' knowledge but parents were unable to insist on return;

4) **Pupil** was absent for no apparent reason with parents' knowledge;

5) **Pupil** was absent for other reasons;

6) Mixed catgory: where physical illness explained 50% or less of the absence – one other category to be indicated.

The education welfare officers and the teachers did not adhere strictly to the guidelines for the completion of the questionnaire and the simplification to six categories or combination of categories proved unacceptable as, in practice, ten or more were used.

When the sample had been selected from the questionnaire returns a letter advising parents of the purpose of the study and how it was to be carried out was sent. This letter aimed at assuring parents of the confidentiality of their involvement and the value of their co-operation. It also provided a means of introduction for the interviewer.

The semi-structured interview was chosen as the appropriate vehicle for the research, as it provided an opportunity to obtain qualitative as well as quantitative data. It was hoped that by adopting this approach the interviewees would have the opportunity to influence the structure and nature of the interview. The data obtained from the predetermined questions permitted an analysis of parent and pupil responses and a comparison between them. The open-ended part of the interview was designed to allow parents and pupils to say something about their perceptions of school and schooling which might permit new dimensions of understanding to emerge. Parents and pupils were asked directly about their attitudes to and experience of school and about absence from school. Questions in the parent interview schedule were paralleled by questions in the pupil interview.

The course of the parent interview was often indicated by what the parent wanted to say. Sometimes the memories and impressions of their own education or general conversation about the family provided a good starting point. Occasionally an opinion was held strongly and needed expressing immediately. A small number of parents proved either so expansive or so reticent that it was difficult to complete the formal schedule. At the close of the interview each parent was asked for permission to include their child in the study and for an interview to be conducted with the pupil was carried out with the parent present but this was felt to be unproductive and was not repeated.

The pupil interview generally began with the identification of the interviewer as someone not connected with authority in or out of school and an assurance of the complete confidentiality of the information imparted. Pupils were on the whole less likely to dictate the format of the interview than their parents had been.

Table 13.1 Absentees by School and Area

			No. on roll Year IV+V	Illness	Condoned Absence	Other Categories	Total Absent
N	B	M	231	51	0	7	58
N	C	C	272	40	5	16	61
S	G	M	154	10	7	8	25
S	C	C	317	39	2	18	59
E	B	C	149	15	14	7	36
E	G	C	190	16	8	7	31
W	B	M	Not Supplied	Not Supplied	7	6	13
W	G	M	167	"	2	8	10
					45	77	293
						122	

KEY
N	North	B	Boys	C	Controlled
S	South	G	Girls	M	Maintained
E	East	C	Co-educational		
W	West				

Table 13.2 Parents Included in Sample

			Excluded by EWO	Contacted by letter	Unable to take part	Refused	Unable to gain entry
N	B	M	0	8	0	1	3
N	C	C	2	12	1	2	1
S	G	M	1	7	1	1	0
S	C	C	0	11	1	1	1
E	B	C	3	13	1	4	0
E	G	C	1	9	1	0	0
W	B	M	1	12	0	1	3
W	G	M	0	9	2	1	1
			8	81	7	11	9

KEY
N	North	B	Boys	C	Controlled
S	South	G	Girls	M	Maintained
E	East	c	Co-educational		
W	West				

Table 13.3   Pupils Included in Sample

			Interviews with parents	Pupils excluded by parents	Easter leavers who missed interview	Absentees who missed interview	Interviews with pupils
N	B	M	4	0	0	1	3
N	C	C	8	0	2	4	3
S	G	M	5	0	0	0	5
S	C	C	8	1	0	0	7
E	B	C	8	0	0	3	6
E	G	C	8	0	0	0	8
W	B	M	8	0	1	4	3
W	G	M	5	0	1	2	3
			54	1	4	14	38

The schools

Table 13.1 illustrates the wide variation between the schools in their estimated levels of justified and unjustified absence. While it seems likely that this distribution reflects ambiguities in the categories and the difficulty of assigning pupils' absence to them, inevitably it must be influenced by the subjective judgements of educational welfare officers and teachers.

The schools approached the subject of the study, and their involvement in it, with caution. This attitude was in contrast to the assent readily obtained from officers of the Belfast Education and Library Board and the Maintained Schools Commission. It was felt that the mechanics of carrying out the interviews might interfere with the running of the school and there was a real fear that parents might become alienated and hostile as a result of the study. It also appeared that schools had learned to regard attendance as a measure of 'effectiveness', in an informal sense and that they were anxious to forestall any potentially detrimental findings. The social problems in their respective catchment areas, the justified or unjustified reputations of other schools, the rationale informing their inclusion in the survey, a suspicion that inclusion reflected upon their own reputation were all topics discussed with principals and teachers at some length. As with the education welfare service once their fears were allayed all those involved were supportive. It emerged during the study that individual schools practised different interpretations of the regulations relating to absenteeism. In one school a pupil might be 'struck' from the register after the twenty-first consecutive day of absence, whereas in another, this was regarded as impractical, as many pupils could disappear from the rolls. Suspension was rare in some schools, commonplace in others; where suspension recurred parents were likely to express feelings of embarrassment, frustration and hostility towards particular members of staff rather than the school as a whole. Moreover, for our purposes, the status of the absence of a suspended pupil was ambiguous. It was unclear whether the absence of the pupil was simply the period pending reinstatement, whether this period was prolonged as parents become more apathetic or whether the activities of pupils during such a period could be regarded as 'condoned'.

Some schools pursued the absences of non-exam fifth years vigorously, others did not. There was also some evidence that the absences of able pupils were seen as legitimate, while that of their less able peers was viewed with some suspicion. A brother and sister going to separate schools – he a prefect doing 'O' levels, she of much lower ability – were both identified as 'condoned absentees'.

The boy's absence was regarded by the principal as legitimate and not excessive and thus his inclusion in the study was greeted with some surprise, while that of his sister was accepted readily. It would appear that the interpretation of schools, of administrative procedures, and their perceptions of the significance of the pupil's absence, do themselves play a part in sustaining certain patterns of attendance.

The parents

Although parents expressed some doubts as to the value of their own education their positive attitude to education and the importance of it for their children was surprising (Table 13.4). Claiming to have been regular attenders themselves, they were on the whole dissatisfied with their child's poor attendance but were inclined to believe that their son or daughter disliked school and to accept the inevitable consequence of that dislike (Table 13.5). Seventy per cent of parents claimed to know whether or not their son or daughter was at school, and also to insist on attendance. Most children were said to be a home, involved in work of some kind or at leisure (Table 13.6) when not at school.

Table 13.4   Parents' and Pupils' Responses to Schooling

Question	Response	Pupil	Parent
Time spent in school useful?	Yes	40%	43%
Is it important to go to school?	Yes	68%	91%
How often did/do you go to school?	Always	8%	80%
Does pupil like school?	Yes	34%	31%
Would parent know if pupil was not at school?	Yes	84%	70%
Would parents insist on pupils' attendance at school?	Yes	55%	80%

Table 13.5   Parents' and Pupils' Accounts of Pupils' Reaction to School

	Parents	Pupils
Like	31%	34%
Dislike	64%	40%
Indifferent	5%	25%

Table 13.6   Breakdown of Pupils' Activities

	Female	Male
Work	24%	6%
Caring	33%	6%
Leisure	29%	56%
Away from home	10%	32%
No unjustified absence	4%	0

Relationships with their child's school were generally regarded by parents as satisfactory in that the schools were approachable. More than half, 54%, had had direct contact with the school during the previous year. A few did express a wish for easier access (Table 13.7).

Table 13.7   Parents' Perception of School

Pupils attendance 'not as good as it should be	70%
Some contact with school this year	54%
More contact wanted	20%
Happy to discuss problems with school	70%

Half the parents referred to one or more peceived sources of stress in their family lives (Table 13.8).

Table 13.8   Unsolicited Information from Parents about Family Circumstances

Death	0%
Illness or injury	20%
One parent family	4%
Unemployment	5%
Other	2%
More than one	18%
Not specified	52%

The pupils

Like their parents the pupils appeared to view education as a good thing but expressed reservations about the value of it for them as individuals. Only 40% (Table 13.4) of the pupils actually felt that their attendance at school would have any pay off for them. Ninety per cent acknowledged their poor attendance, and 66% disliked or were indifferent to school (Tables 13.9 and 13.5).

When pressed boredom and particular subjects were given as reasons for not attending school. More than half the pupils felt they had no-one with whom they could discuss it. However only 18% actually wished to change school (Table 13.9).

When absent most were involved in some kind of leisure activity or the care of a relative – smaller numbers were away from home or involved in work, 19% and 16% respectively. Boys were significantly more likely to be at leisure. Pupils saw themselves involved in work less than their parents did and significantly more perceived themselves as 'caring' (Table 13.6).

Table 13.9   Pupils' Responses to School

Absent when not ill	90%
Someone to talk to in school about absence	36½%
Prefer a different school	18%
Question: Why don't you want to go to school?	
Boredom	26%
Subjects	24%
Teachers	15%
Other	16%
Does not apply	18%

Over half the parents – 55% – were characterised as making some form of protest about the absence (Table 13.4).

In the open-ended questions two-thirds of the parents and pupils reflected an instrumental, means-ends concept of education – did it help you to read, write or get a job? However for many failure at school was not regarded as the fault of the school but rather as more dependent on the individual and his background. Only 18% of the pupils expressed a desire to change schools (Table 13.9). The predominant feeling was that a change of school would make no difference to their attitude to school – 'They're all the same, aren't they?'. They would, apparently, be bored (26%), dislike subjects (24%) and teachers (15%) no matter where they were (Table 13.9). The inability of their school to motivate and interest them and to provide them with the skills and knowledge which they perceived would be valuable in later life did not prevent over 90% of parents and over two-thirds of the pupils expressing a positive attitude towards the importance of attendance at school. This suggests that it is not education as such which the pupils are rejecting but specific aspects of what schools offer to their pupils. It was argued in the introduction that if what we do to our pupils in schools is a variable in their attendance at school then the view of the pupil of what happens in school must be accepted as legitimate. If then they are rejecting elements as irrelevant and inappropriate to their real lives it becomes necessary for schools to respond.

The fourth and fifth year less able project (DENI) was an attempt at such a response. However it is not always the curriculum of the school which is the important variable in non-attendance and the activities that pupils are involved in out of school may also be a contributory factor and in some cases provide an adequate reason for staying away

Table 13.10   Open-ended Questions – Pupil Interview

Question: Do you think the time you spend in school will be any good to you in the future? Try to give reasons for your answer.	
Pupils related their answer to:	
Relevance of subjects to daily life	37%
Employment	24%
Qualifications	8%
Don't know	11%
Question: It it important to go to school? Try to give reasons for your answer.	
No reasons given	29%
Basics (i.e. literacy, numeracy)	18%
'To learn things'	11%
'For an education'	8%

from school. This is best illustrated by the experience of some of the individual pupils in the study.

Charles did not like 'lessons' nor sitting in the same room for long periods of time but he could, in his eyes and hers, legitimately use the fact of his mother's physical and psychological incapacity as a reason for not attending school.

Kim and her mother perceived Kim's non-attendance from different perspectives.They both agreed that although Kim could cope at school she had hated it from when she left primary school. However mother saw this as the reason she stayed away from school and said that when Kim was at home she was either 'sleeping' or 'visiting her grandmother' but not helping her. Kim, on the other hand, claimed that her absence was entirely due to her mother's illness (she had arthritis) and although her mother told her to go to school she did not like to.

Marie saw her non-attendance as 'because of the school' and one teacher in particular. Her mother also perceived the school as unsympathetic and responsible for her daughter's attitude. The dislike of a specific teacher appears to be a more important variable than the content of a subject. Even where a subject was given as a reason for a dislike of school it was often evident from the response that it was how the subject was taught not the content of it that gave rise to the dislike.

Where suspension had been incurred, as in Marie's case, the degree of frustration and bitterness expressed was considerable and often the school was perceived as personally threatening so that the parents neither desired nor would have accepted greater contact with the school.

Policy implications

It would seem from both the quantitative and qualitative data obtained from this study that responses which are essentially curricular based are insufficient to make any impression on those pupils who habitually absent themselves from school with their parent's knowledge and for no apparent reason. However why these pupils do this is a highly complex problem involving a unique interaction between each pupil, his parents and his home, and his teachers and his school.

A number of models can be drawn from this study which might help to explain this interaction which could be called the process of absenteeism.

In the first model a pupil may dislike school because of his/her attitudes to a particular teacher, a subject or event, but very rarely, if this study is indicative of the general, the curriculum as a whole and may decide not to go to school. The parents, although not liking the absence from school, feel helpless in the face of an intransigent teenager and after some protest yield to the inevitable. One mother verbalised the feeling of helplessness of such a situation.

> You can only do so much – then it's up to the child.

A pupil described how she wore her parents' opposition down through sheer persistence:

> They keep saying you'll have to go back – but I keep on and then they give in.

In such situations, where the parents are 'unable to insist on return' (survey questionnaire) it is understandable that schools might feel the time and effort expended in order to get a fifteen or sixteen year-old back to school is excessive and unproductive. Thus the absence becomes persistent, consented to by home and school.

A second model incorporates the failure and consequent low self esteem in the school environment which is often associated with an expression of boredom or dislike of a teacher or subject. Some of the pupils in the study expressed this in terms of the school's inability to 'teach you anything' or keep them interested and motivated 'you get threw out anyway'. If school has nothing to offer you and appears uninterested then there is no point in going.

Thirdly, both parents and pupils emphasised the importance of outcomes such as certain competences like reading and writing or the ability to 'get a job' but were unable to articulate the value going to school had for them. This seems to suggest that perceptions of 'relevance' and 'value' were confined to specific personal contexts. Schools, on the other hand, view 'relevance' and 'value' from a wider perspective based on the greatest good for the greatest number. Parents and pupils do not relate as individuals to this concept and this may be a contributing factor in the apparent reluctance of parents to make or sustain contact with school and when required to do so, as in cases of suspension, they feel embarrassed and threatened. It is important that this feeling be set in the context of parents' and pupils' apparent acceptance of the individual's responsibility for his own success or failure and the lack of desire to change schools. If one school has little to offer it is unlikely that another will be very different. In the words of one of the pupils:

It wouldn't make any difference, they're all the same.

The incompatibility of the pupil, his home and the school is accepted by pupils and although parents protest sincerely about poor attendance they also accept it.

These models of the process of absenteeism from school are not mutually exclusive nor do they reflect all aspects of the process. However such models provide a means of interpreting absenteeism and an opportunity of devising appropriate response strategies. In situations where pupils express dislike of individual teachers or subjects it is often a reflection of how the individual pupil is treated. He dislikes the lack of control of his own behaviour and the authority of the school to dictate what he should do, when he should do it and how it is to be done. These pupils demonstrate in their lives outside school an ability to take decisions for themselves and sometimes for others; and even cope in stressful situations unfamiliar to many teachers. Is there not an argument then for schools treating pupils as individuals and developing this capacity to decide for themselves?

Often absentees are labelled and stigmatised as failures because they reject a regime which is alien to them as individuals and to their lifestyles. A radical response to this might be to contract with each pupil an agreed amount of work over the course of an academic term. This contract would specify an amount of work, how it would be taught and assessed, a required number of days attendance and the sanction to be imposed for non-completion of the contract. It would be agreed to and signed by pupils and teachers. The contract could be reviewed at set intervals by pupil and teachers and satisfactory progress recorded or appropriate sanctions applied – this would apply equally to both pupil and teacher.

This would allow the pupil to take responsibility for and be involved in the process of his own learning. There is already some evidence on the practice of such a process. Rutter (1979) in '15,000 Hours' suggested that schools which adopted a policy of pupil involvement could be regarded as more effective. More recently the ILEA Junior School Project has investigated a school system which specifies clear academic and social goals, an agreement about order and discipline, a higher expectation of success, a closer monitoring of progress to provide feedback on difficulties and variety in both teaching and learning strategies. Such a response from schools to their pupils would of necessity have implications for the curriculum. The quest for relevance, motivation and interest would be mutual and real. The ability to read and write may well be linked with the development of the self, citizenship, political awareness and aspects of work and leisure rather than to the traditional collection of accepted disciplines. The boredom, which was often suggested by pupils as an explanation of the continuing absence, would be offset by a curriculum that reflects the contemporary world of the young adult. The learning would be self-programmed and evaluated by both learner and teacher. Attendance would be contractual on a set number of days but beyond that would be determined by the pupil's own wish.

All the models given of the process of absenteeism and the outline responses indicated would necessitate a highly developed counselling service which would ensure that pupils always had someone to talk to. Many in the study indicated that they felt there was no sympathetic ear available. This service would have to be easily accessible to vulnerable young adults and be perceived as being useful and provide complete confidentiality.

The interaction between the pupil, his school and his home is always complex but never more so than in cases where the pupil habitually absents himself from school and this is with parental knowledge. Any school response to such persistent absenteeism must then incorporate the development of meaningful ways of involving parents in the education of their children. The barriers which many parents of non-attenders feel exist between them and the school must be broken down and a new partnership defined.

To bring about such change would require a fundamental change in attitude by both parents and teachers. The parents have shown that they believe that for schools to matter they must lead the way and show they care.

Chapter 14

YTP – Some Lessons for Education?

Jean Whyte
(Lecturer, Trinity College, Dublin)

Introduction

The Youth Training Programme was initiated in Northern Ireland in September 1982. An ambitious and expensive project, its aim was to lay the foundation for a skilled flexible workforce while also helping sixteen and seventeen year-olds to make the transition from school to working life. Since one of its target groups is sixteen year-old school leavers, for whom it provides a guaranteed year of skills training, work experience and further education, any study of the progamme or of those entering it will offer a unique opportunity to examine the outcomes and consider the potential of the educational system for those young people who leave school as early as is legally possible. There have been several such opportunities since the initiation of the programme. These included the *YTP Refusers Survey* (PPRU, 1983) *YTP Leavers Survey* (1982 entrants; PPRU, 1984) *Are They Being Served?* (1983 entrants, NICER/DED, 1985) and the *YTP Cohort Study* (1984 entrants; PPRU, 1986–88). Since the studies were all carried out in the context of the Youth Training Programme, a brief outline of that provision is necessary to introduce relevant terminology.

The Youth Training Programme

The Northern Ireland Youth Training Programme represents the culmination of a series of attempts to cater for the needs of young people in Northern Ireland. The programme is provided by partnerships organised among community workshops, employers, (including Industrial Training Boards) Colleges of Further Education and Government Training Centres. It offers full-time training to those sixteen and seventeen year-olds not yet in employment, additional training to young people in employment and increased vocational preparation to young people who remain in full-time education. Entry is through assessment and interview by careers officers.

Research studies

While none of the studies cited had the delineation of educational issues among its primary aims, they all sought data related to the educational experiences of YTP entrants which it was felt would have a bearing on their subsequent choices and fortunes. The findings were generally consistent across cohorts and across studies as will be seen below. The NICER/DED study (Whyte *et al.*, 1985), however, obtained more information of relevance to the question under consideration here since the data collected were related not only to trainees' past experiences in education but also, and in considerable detail, to further education within the YTP. The study followed a cohort of 921 young people, representing 1 in 6 of the total YTP guaranteed year intake in September 1983, until after they had completed their guaranteed year of training in December 1984. As well as a series of questionnaires the trainees completed attainment and psychological tests and information was also obtained through structured interviews and questionnaires from employers, GTC managers, FE college principals, lecturers, instructors, supervisors, tutors and careers officers who were involved with the trainees in the sample.

Chapter outline

One of the first concerns of the NICER study was to establish critical characteristics of the young people which would be relevant in assessing their reaction to YTP. These were mainly characteristics which should have been targeted by the education system in which they had spent eleven years. They are reported in the first part of the chapter and will be of interest especially to those responsible for educational services to 11–16 year-olds.

Information was also sought on the rationale, content and methods of the educational element of YTP. Set against the critical characteristics of the young people on entering YTP, this gives rise to the second set of findings which will be of relevance to those in the further education sector concerned with 16–17 year-olds. The final part of the chapter identifies issues arising from the findings and suggests some avenues worth exploring by those, especially in the education system, who are concerned with the future prospects of young people in Northern Ireland.

Characteristics of young people entering YTP

Three categories of characteristics relevant to educational experience were observable from the data gathered:

general knowledge and basic communication skills;
employment-related skills and attitudes;
personal and social skills and attitudes.

General knowledge and basic communication skills

Subjective impressions usually suggest that many sixteen year-old unemployed school leavers are low achievers. This was supported by the finding that 54% of the sample had either not attempted to obtain or had not obtained credit for any externally validated certificates at all before leaving school. This figure is higher than any others obtained in studies of school leavers in Northern Ireland and may have been sample related since it is based on a sample selected from those actually starting a YTP course and is representative of the proportions in different schemes. The PPRU figure for those unqualified entering YTP is 29% based on a cohort sample including eventual non-YTP entrants, followed since before they left school. This figure is probably also sample related since it was drawn from a school-going population. The true extent of educational disadvantage among certain sections of the population is probably concealed when overall statistics are considered.

One of the underlying causes of this poor showing in the qualifications stakes, a cause which had serious implications apart from the lack of externally validated certificates, is probably the poor level of attainment in basic communication skills typical of many in this group.
The courses in Table 14.1 were 'mainstream' YTP. Courses for groups with special needs were provided by the FE sector in 1983–84 as follows:
YW = Youthways; LA = courses for the less able, with a variety of names such as Routeways; BE = Basic Education. Additional courses known as 'Pathfinder' courses are offered in 1988–89 for young people with mainly physical handicaps.

While a considerable range of attainment and variation in the distribution of scores was found within each scheme for the standardised tests administered at the beginning of the NICER/DED project, the results showed that some schemes had a higher proportion of low attainers than others. In the Community Workshops (also known as

Table 14.1   Percentage of Low Scores in Reading, Arithmetic and Vocabulary by YTP Scheme
(Whyte *et al.*, 1985)

	GTC	WPC	WPU	EBS	YW	LA	BE
No.=	224	247	164	137	106	26	17
Reading (NS6) R.A. 11	17	24	35	20	36	91	67
Arithmetic Score 25%	16	7	28	12	19	84	27
Vocabulary (EPVT) X=100; SS 85	52	52	71	49	69	96	86

Note: GTC = Government Training Centres
WPC = Work Preparation Centres based in FE colleges
WPU = Work Preparation Units (also know as Community Workshops).

Work Preparation Units: WPUs) a sampled 35% of the trainees entering had reading ages of less than 11 years and 28% achieved scores of under 25% in a simple test of the 4 rules of number. Vocabulary scores were low overall compared to British norms.

These scores do not, however, tell the whole story. A considerable amount of underachievement was suggested by the finding that 38% of those who had left school with no externally validated certificate had nevertheless achieved reading scores in the highest range and should have been capable of examination success in some area of study (Table 14.2).

Issues for discussion

These findings show a need for the educational system to look critically at the methods, materials and content employed with 11-16 year-olds and to evaluate the objectives in terms of minimum standards of achievement expected of school leavers. The PPRU and NICER studies all found that young people with pre-YTP, i.e. school-gained qualifications were more likely to find employment post-YTP than their less well qualified or unqualified peers.

Table 14.2   Reading Age by Examinations Passed

(Whyte *et al.*, 1985)

Reading Age	No Exams	RSA	CSE (Gr 2, 3, 4)	1–3 O Levels (or CSE I)	4+ O Levels (or CSE I)
11	39%	21%	16%	4%	2%
12–15	23%	19%	22%	12%	0%
15+	38%	59%	62%	84%	98%

Employment related knowledge and attitudes

Trainees themselves identified a need for vocational skills as a reason for joining YTP and so did careers officers. Employers mentioned job-related attitudes as being essential, but lacking in young people; they were not concerned about skills which they felt could be acquired on the job. While many trainees appeared to be aware of this need, it did not play a major role for the majority in deciding on a specific scheme or centre. This decision is made while they are still attending school, so the researchers investigated the possibility that information on courses offering these skills may not have been readily available to them there. It was found, however, that they were more likely to have been given information about YTP than about other options and in addition a range of sources was identified including careers officers, jobmarkets, school friends, television, parents, newspapers. In short, they appeared to be adequately informed.

But throughout the careers officers' responses, there were many references to the need for better liaison with schools. Some careers officers reported problems particularly with principals and 44% suggested that principals did not have a positive attitude towards YTP. In contrast only 12% had come across careers teachers with a negative approach to the programme although a further 15% said that some careers teachers were helpful while others were not. Schools appeared to be more likely to inform pupils about GTC courses than about some of the others available, especially full-time FE courses. There may have been an element of the numbers game at work here (McCartney and Whyte, 1984).

Trainees attitudes towards employment were very positive. Over 70% had applied for jobs before joining YTP and their employment aspirations spanned a wide range of levels and occupations. However, when aspirations were related to data on ability and achievements, it was obvious that many lacked an appreciation of the fact that basic skills such as literacy and numeracy are required for almost any type of employment.

Summary

These findings indicate that schools are providing job and training-related information to a satisfactory level on the whole, though there are exceptions; the plea for better liaison with careers officers and for perhaps some work on attitudes among principals merits attention. There is a hint of excessive concern for the institution over the individual needs of pupils in what could be perceived as unwillingness to promote the attractions of rival establishments such as FE colleges offering full-time courses. On the other hand, schools do appear to be imbuing pupils with a positive attitude towards employment – though, as will be seen below, this may be somewhat of a 'rebound' situation.

Personal and social skills and attitudes

Attention was drawn to the needs of the young people in this area of development, and it was seen as a priority by almost all the tutors, managers, instructors and supervisors in contact with them. Specific examples of needs mentioned by employers were those of self-confidence and flexibility. Careers officers' assessments of the young people included judgements about appearance and disposition and suggested that a sizeable core of trainees had need of specific help in these areas. Unfavourable ratings for appearance were given to 37% of boys and 31% of girls; while for disposition, 40% of boys and 45% of the girls were unfavourably assessed.

A further underlying trait which probably had wider repercussions for personal and social skills was an apparent feeling of insecurity, possibly based on lack of self-knowledge and lack of skill in assessing facts objectively; areas of experience they had possibly missed in school or from which they had certainly not benefited, if they were available. This emerged from the responses of the trainees when asked why they had selected a particular YTP centre. The reason given by the highest percentage in all mainstream schemes (except EBS) was that of closeness to home – nothing to do with the content, skills offered or aims of the courses, even though many of the young people had claimed to be interest in job-related skills. This could, at the very least, have had far-reaching consequences in the context of YTP, for, according to some careers officers, many young people made a wrong choice of scheme by basing their choice on closeness to home and the presence of friends. Their willingness to accept almost whatever was proposed to them as a training programme could be seen as a further reflection of the same trait.

The desire to cling to the familiar was seen also in the reluctance of some trainees at an early stage of the programme, to attend FE colleges which were off their usual beaten track or where they would have been participating in classes with groups of socio-cultural backgrounds different from their own. Similarly, their reluctance to move out of their own areas for work-experience or leisure-type activities limited the opportunities available to them. It is undeniable of course, that in the context of Northern Ireland in the 1980s, particularly in parts of Belfast, they may have grown up with reasons for this behaviour related to the violence of the 'troubles', indelibly marked in their consciousness.

A further relevant attitude expressed by the young people was in relation to school itself. A high percentage (56%) had chosen to enter YTP because they disliked school and 36% would not consider full-time FE courses on the grounds that they were too like school. This negative attitude may well be a reflection of a more general negative attitude towards the self in that it constitutes a rejection of socially acceptable means of advancing one's development, it may also, ultimately, reflect a negative attitude towards society and its demands. This study found evidence of the failure of the education system to recognise and encourage potential and to make young people aware of their own strengths. It is possible that relevant weaknesses were not offered assistance in an acceptable context. The result was rejection by the young people of the system, and the development of non-constructive attitudes which coloured their decision-making.

Initiatives for discussion

Can the education system have a role to play in the development of more positive attitudes and characteristics? It is likely that those found by the NICER/DED study are due to a multiplicity of factors related to the home, and to the general cultural-religious and socio-economic circumstances of individuals and their families as well as to the school. It is undeniable, however, that personal and social skills and attitudes contribute to the achievement of potential in the individual – an area of primary concern for the education system. It could be seen, therefore, as the responsibility of the school to initiate studies investigating these relationships and exploring ways of improving the self-image and self-confidence of young people as well as the consequences of change for these individuals.

The educational element within the guaranteed year of YTP

The educational element within the guaranteed year of YTP can be seen to be potentially of great importance to the young people who present themselves with needs such as those outlined in the previous section of this paper. The Youth Training Programme aimed in fact to help individuals through the development of appropriate curricula. The NICER/DED study investigated the means by which the curriculum was developed and the extent to which it appeared to have helped the young people by obtaining information on the following aspects:

> the extent to which the curriculum was needs-based or built on existing resources;
> the degree by which the curriculum was decided through negotiation;
> the nature of the content actually provided;
> the reactions of the young people to the educational element.

Information was sought in these areas with the aim of determining the degree to which the education element was responding to the needs of the young people and thereby making a positive contribution to the overall YTP curriculum.

The basis for the curriculum

(a) Institutional level

Instruction in the FE college, usually on one day each week, was intended to complement the experiences provided by the other elements of the scheme and also to cater for individual needs in such areas as communication skills, and social and life skills.

Consultation and co-ordination between providers of other schemes and the further education colleges would seem to be an essential pre-requisite to drawing up the curriculum. When providers were interviewed by the research team, however, three of the GTC managers in the sample of six said that there had been no independent consultation about the content of the education element for their trainees. The curriculum had in fact been designed by a DED/DENI team which included FE and GTC representatives but was possibly a little remote from those dealing with trainees every day.

Four of the eleven WPUs in the sample and a quarter of the employers interviewed from the Employer-Based Schemes (as they were then)
had not been consulted by the local college about the educational
needs of their YTP trainees. In fact, over 40% of employers said that
they had problems in arranging a suitable education element. This
bleak picture was slightly lightened by a few providers who stated that
they enjoyed excellent relationships with the local college and had full
co-operation arranging suitable courses for their trainees.

(b) Trainer level

But even if the broad outlines of the curriculum were designated by
people at high levels, perhaps those on the ground had some discretion
in filling in the details and thereby matching to some extent the
observed needs of trainees. The situation was found to vary according
to provider. Staff in FE colleges were more likely to have courses
planned by the head of department or by the course tutor and head of
department or by a team, although a small proportion could decide
aspects of the course for themselves. Courses in most schemes (apart
from WPUs) were, however, decided in advance of meeting the trainees. Published schemes of work were used more by some groups (e.g.
joinery tutors in FE) than by others (WPU supervisors). In general the
courses offered appeared to depend on resources already available in
the various colleges and on courses already being taught at different
levels.

Social and life skills tutors seemed to have a different system of working. They were attached to FE colleges but provided teaching in this
area for all other providers and they appeared to have greater freedom
to decide for themselves on the course content for individual groups.
In some cases where a number of social and life skills tutors were based
in the same college, a team discussion approach had been developed;
most of them also consulted the trainees extensively. Constraints on
course content emanating from a curriculum committee on which they
had only indirect representation were, however, mentioned by social
and life skills tutors in one location.

(c) Availability of background knowledge

While it did not appear to the researchers that the procedures adopted
for the development of the curriculum except in the case of some social
and life skills tutors, allowed for the possibility that needs and experiences of trainees might be taken into account, it was possible that the

discretion given to informed and qualified individuals in making decisions about the curriculum could be seen as fulfilling the spirit of YTP, especially if the deliberations were based on adequate information about the young people.

It was found in this study, however, that while individual assessments had been carried out by careers officers for all entrants to YTP neither these assessments nor ratings on the CASPA scale nor the reasons for the ratings were made available to scheme organisers. In fact, in the vast majority of schemes, no prior information beyond the trainee's name (and sometimes not even that much) was made available before the arrival of the individual to the centre to which he or she was seeking admission. No formal assessments were carried out in the majority of schemes (apart from GTCs who had a standard assessment form) and information about specific needs was gleaned gradually through interview and performance on the various tasks undertaken, sometimes during an assessment period (e.g. in the community workshops).

(d) Trainee consultation

In the absence of baseline assessments, a final possible way of aiming for the ideal YTP educational curriculum might have involved consulting the trainees. Whether this had happened was determined in part by asking whether trainees had any choice in the selection of education courses and any say in the actual course they followed. This kind of consultation was envisaged by YTP planners as essential for the young people's development and as part of the process of negotiation which was to be practised at all levels.

There was some variation in the attitudes of providers towards the possibility of negotiation on the education element of the curriculum. The majority of community workshops allowed some negotiation on certain aspects of the education element and this was confirmed by 47% of workshop trainees who said that they had been consulted. Four of the six colleges of further education in the sample said that they permitted negotiation on some elements of the course and this was apparent to 40% of FE trainees; GTCs had no mechanism for permitting negotiation with trainees about the education element.

Tutors were asked if they ever negotiated with trainees, what the topic of negotiation was and what form the negotiation took. More social and life skills tutors (83%) than others said that they negotiated with trainees; those who were least likely to negotiate were FE tutors, whether clerical (50% negotiated) or joinery (20%). Those who were more likely to negotiate were WPU staff (more than 78%). Negotiation

centred on the content of the course especially for social and life skills
tutors, but also on project work, recreation, and sometimes on rules,
regulations and the duration of different activities.

Issues for discussion

These findings on the procedures adopted in determining the educational curriculum for YTP trainees suggested that the spirit of YTP had
not yet had an impact in this area. There probably was a great gap
between what had been normal autocratic procedures within education
– procedures which had possibly contributed to the problems mani-
fested by the young people – and the more open climate of discussion
and negotiation now being advocated. But perhaps in spite of this, the
content development was relevant and the methods and materials
appropriate?

Content of the education element

The education element of the Youth Training Programme was provided for most of the trainees on a one day per week basis in a college
of further education. When trainees were asked to state what they were
being taught in the education classes, the responses were categorised as
follows:

> Subjects related to work skills – 60%
> Subjects related to job aspirations of individuals – 58%
> Literacy and numeracy – 32%
> Social and life skills – 28%

The latter included communication skills, social skills, interpersonal
skills, personal development and health education. Over 60% of all
trainees had learnt about applying for jobs and about interviews. They
were also exposed to information and skills of a general kind in the discussions and debates organised by social and life skills tutors on matters
of interest to their individual groups.

(a) Specific skills practised

In further questions trainees were asked to indicate whether they had
been given opportunities to practise specific basic skills (as described in
YTP policy documents) during the various components of their
courses. The responses showed that particular skills appeared to be

favoured by different settings – the centre where work skills were taught, the education centre or the work experience setting. The ten basic skills listed were then rank-ordered and the results showed that 'listening and talking' was the skill given most practice in the edcuational setting (Whyte *et al.*, p. 84).

The skills on which schemes tended to place little emphasis were similar. They included computers, reading, problem-solving tasks, tasks involving tools and equipment, writing and using hands to organise materials. This meant that trainees who needed help in those particular skills would have had problems in locating a suitable scheme and that the FE colleges were not in fact checking on gaps which needed to be filled. These findings were supported by those of the PPRU cohort study a year later.

Effectiveness of the education element

This issue was explored by asking trainees about specific skills and by asking them in a general way what they had learnt.

The responses showed that the education setting helped most in learning interpersonal skills such as 'getting on with others', and 'listening and talking' for all groups, though GTC and FE groups also learned about computers in this setting. On the other hand, FE colleges providing the education element were least successful in helping reading, 'organising own work' and 'using hands to organise materials'. This was perhaps not surprising since they appeared to spend so little time on these practical skills as seen above.

Trainees were asked in an open-ended question if they had learned anything new from the education classes in their centres and at the tech. Responses varied somewhat according to the type of scheme with positive responses ranging from 68% (GTC) to 35% (LA). Trainees from the GTCs were the most positive about the usefulness of the education classes with about 78% of them describing the FE courses as useful or very useful, while 44% of trainees from community workshops, than from any other type of scheme, thought that the education classes were 'of no use' and 30% of these trainees said that they had learnt 'nothing' from the education element.

Social and life skills

An identifiable social and life skills element was provided for all trainees. Most of the trainees thought it was useful and the majority thought that the teaching was acceptable with only 6% rating it as 'poor'. Trainees on day release were the most critical. Social and life skills appears to have been integrated most satisfactorily for those on full-time YTP courses with FE especially the less able students – a higher percentage of them (48%) than of other groups could see the relevance of social and life skills to other parts of the course. The percentages were very low for other groups; the highest of these was EBS trainees (33%) who appeared to be the only day-release trainees to find the social and life skills element to be related to their needs to any extent.

Why so negative?

It might be thought that the reason why particular groups did not feel they had benefited from the educational element in YTP was because it was geared to the specific needs of other groups. In fact the main reason for criticism given was that respondents had already covered the material. It would appear, therefore, that there was a mismatch both in terms of level and of content. Possible explanations for these somewhat negative impressions were sought by asking for trainees' opinions on the interest and difficulty level of the subjects studied, their rating of the quality of instruction and their views on the usefulness and relevance of the educational element as a whole.

Interest level

Of mainstream YTP a much higher percentage rated as 'interesting' the work skills and work experience elements than the education elements. The range of those who said the various aspects were interesting was as follows:

English/literacy/communication	42% (GTC) – 63% (FE)
Maths/numeracy	33% (FE) – 57% (EBS)
Social and life skills	60% (WPU) – 75% (EBS)
Other subjects	53% (GTC) – 83% (FE)

Difficulty level

The difficulty level of the skills and subjects taught does not appear to have been a problem unless it was that the material was not stimulating enough. In the second questionnaire fewer than 4% rated the skills they were being taught as 'difficult' and between 17% and 27% rated them as 'easy'. As far as the education element was concerned, up to 29% (depending on the scheme) rated the English and maths as easy and up to 17% rated them as difficult. The social and life skills and other sub-jects seem to have been better pitched with up to 20% rating them as easy and less than 10% rating them as difficult. The education element appeared to be similar to the skills training element on this dimension as fewer than 4% rated the skills they were being taught as 'difficult' and between 17% and 27% rated them as 'easy'. It was interesting to note that the community workshop trainees were at the extremes of the range for most of these variables thereby indicating the mixed-ability nature of these groups and the problems there must be in making pro-vision for them.

Quality of instruction

The instruction level may of course depend on the quality of instruc-tion that is given. Trainees were asked on several occasions to rate the instruction. It emerged that fewer than 50% of any scheme rated the further eduation instruction as a whole as 'good' on a scale which included good, OK and poor. In order to ascertain whether this rating was due to a generally negative attitude this was compared with ratings of other elements such as work skills instruction. The finding that the skills training instruction was rated 'good' by between 50% and 70% of trainees suggests that trainees were discriminating and that the quality of instruction in the education element was perceived as lower down the scale.

Likes and dislikes

Education classes did not fare well under this heading compared to other aspects of the courses. When they were asked about the education classes, between 26% and 44% mentioned specific classes they had liked in different subject areas, but 52% of GTC trainees said that they had liked 'nothing' and this was true also for between 15% and 24% of the other trainees. Other questions elicited similar responses – all very neg-ative towards education.

Selective effectiveness?

It was possible, however, that the educational element might have been effective for individuals who had a higher degree of disadvantage in the communication skills area or in the personal and social skills area. This did not turn out to be the case for low achievers – those who had no exams on entry to YTP – of whom 54% said that they had learnt nothing to help their reading and writing on YTP, and at the other end of the scale, 65% of those who had some exams said the same thing. The figure was 52% for those in the middle.

On the other hand, those in need of help in personal development do seem to have benefited. When those who had scored high on social competence were compared with those scoring low, more of those who had scored in the 'low' category than in the 'high' category (as determined early in the year) said that they had been helped a lot in the following areas of personal development: getting to know own strengths and weaknesses, growing up, making you more independent, making decisions, improving self-confidence, solving problems, making new friends (this was supported by PPRU findings).

Trainees' views – an aberration?

The trainees' impressions of the education element of YTP seem to have been more negative than positive – was this linked to their general dislike of things educational, a hangover from their days in school or did the adults in contact with them share these impressions to any extent?

Views of careers officers

Careers officers, while acknowledging that they were not adequately informed about day-release classes, felt that they were 'very good' or 'acceptable' for GTC trainees and for those taking examination courses. There may have been some basis in fact for this belief, since in many instances the arrangements for further education of GTC trainees had been worked out over a long period and they had probably developed to a satisfactory level. Arrangements with other providers were just beginning to evolve in a rather unstructured way, as seen above, and only just over 50% of careers officers who replied said that it was even at an acceptable level for any other type of scheme. It was felt by careers officers that there should be more flexibility and more effort to relate the education element to other elements in the Youth Training Programme should be made by employers, WPU, GTC managers and FE principals.

The employers who were interviewed were on the whole very critical of the further education element. They complained of lack of flexibility in the course structure as had been noted by careers officers and asserted that the courses were not related to the work situation, that the young people were bored or unhappy and that the courses lacked variety and were too like school. Similar points were made by WPU managers, in addition they wanted more practical skills taught such as tool care. Some schemes had suffered from lack of adequate liaison and one described the provision as 'chaotic'. It was felt that the lecturers assigned to YTP day-release groups were not always those best suited to the work and that they were not adequately skilled in dealing with the trainees and in recognising their problems.

The GTC managers even mentioned some doubt about whether the content of the courses was entirely appropriate, although some GTCs were quite satisfied with the service they were getting from FE colleges. Problems related to the education element such as keeping track of attendance, arranging transport and coping with intimidation had arisen in some cases. The FE colleges said spontaneously that there were problems sometimes in finding suitable lecturers for each day-release group. This in turn made it difficult to develop syllabus content.

Points to ponder

In summary the only positive finding about the educational element in YTP after all the effort the providers made appears to have been the beneficial effect it was acknowledged to have had on personal and social skills. Psychologically, it may be significant that this was the aspect of development most open to change at this time for the young people. In Maslow's hierarchy of needs (1968, 1970), the need for self-esteem must be satisfied to a certain extent before a person feels free enough to tackle tasks associated with self-actualisation – which in this case could be interpreted loosely as basic reading and writing skills. The question of why young people at this age were in such dire need of having self-esteem built up is one for the 11–16 educators to tackle.

Possible reasons for this result, which could be considered meagre in some responses, although in others it was a very positive one, are best deduced from the suggestions proposed for improving YTP made by participants at all levels.

Suggestions for change and issues for debate

Some of the suggestions for change were related to individuals' percep-tions of their own role in YTP and the way in which their role was related to that of others. We have already seen that the role of trainee was quite well defined and understood both by trainees and by trainers – a person needing training and development, to be consulted sometimes by some people; the roles of the adults concerned with placing and training the young people were not so well defined. Perceptions of status differential between those involved in different elements of the scheme were a source of some dissatisfaction. These perceptions were fuelled by factors such as differences in the number of trainees per group, the duration of sessions and of course components, the conditions of service in terms of paid teaching and non-teaching hours, and adequacy of equipment and materials, the opportunities for gaining qualifications and experience. Many respondents thought that improvements in these areas for trainers would result in an improvement in the quality of YTP for the young people.

Four specific areas were targeted in the suggestions for improvement made by participants:

(i)   Changes in teaching methods were seen as a priority by many respondents who admitted that they needed help themselves in developing new skills to overcome the difficulties of which they were only too aware in their day-to-day encounters. Some of the difficulties were seen as having their roots in the social and cultural backgrounds of the trainees and even of the trainers, but, others were felt to be due to the educational system and even to the course structure of YTP.

(ii) The second main area in which staff said they needed help was that of the development evaluation of curriculum content, and in addition the skills of collaboration with trainers involved with other elements of the curriculum.

(iii) The third area of need was felt to be that of assessment and evaluation skills – assessment of needs and evaluation of methods, of content, of progress towards meeting needs.

(iv) The fourth general area of need emerged from the attitudes of trainers towards the profiling system in use at that time (1983–84). They appeared to be particularly uncertain in their management and handling of the profiles which involved the development of a positive and trusting relationship with trainees. This was an interesting finding for it suggests a certain lack of personal and social skills in the trainers (who would have come through the educational system some years earlier and with apparently similar outcomes in terms of lack of flexibility and self-confidence as the current trainees).

A further area of concern was voiced in particular by some social and life skills tutors who were, as seen above, in a better position than some of the other people involved in training, as regards the immediate needs of the young people. A strong case was made for a more substantial health education input (elements of which were in fact included in some of the courses) and also for some efforts to be made in providing for the development of cultural and political awareness and understanding among young people. It was thought that opportunities were not being grasped when misunderstandings could be pinpointed and open discussion encouraged about everyday issues affecting Northern Ireland. Tutors with these concerns felt that they themselves lacked the training, experience and confidence to tackle these issues but that they would welcome encouragement to become involved and the support which further professional training could give. There were, however, some tutors who did not see this as part of their role and supervisors and instructors who saw far more of the young people than the formal social and life skills tutors and had even less preparation for tackling these issues than had the FE staff.

The NICER study revealed an overwhelming awareness among participants of the need for greater staff development. This must surely depend on the willingness of the educational sector to make a positive contribution.

Conclusions

Recent studies of sixteen year-old school leavers who joined the Northern Ireland Youth Training Programme revealed serious weaknesses in their preparation for life in terms of basic communication, general knowledge and personal and social life skills and attitudes. In addition many of the young people had left school with strong negative feelings about education. The educational element in YTP was not structured or organised adequately to meet the challenge presented to it although individuals on the ground undoubtedly did what they could within the brief assigned to them. Dissatisfaction may also be seen as underlying the numerous proposals for improvement suggested by participants at every level of the programme.

Neither this finding nor the situation from which it arose is unique to Northern Ireland. Similar problems are being dealt with in a variety of ways elsewhere and have been well documented and evaluated (UNESCO 1987, for example). While Northern Ireland may have some problems specific to the province, and a start has perhaps been made on these by the recent (January 1989) announcement of committees to

consider curricula in the areas of personal, social and cultural awareness, there are examples of good practice in other countries which have
problems in related areas about which those on the ground should be
informed.

The involvement with YTP has shown that the educational system in
Northern Ireland urgently needs to make changes in the knowledge,
attitudes and skills of the educators. This can only be achieved through
opportunities to innovate and evaluate which are well designed and
adequately supported and reported.

Chapter 15

Schools Under Scrutiny

Leslie Caul
(Lecturer, Stranmillis College, Belfast)

If one issue is prevalent in education in Northern Ireland it is that of
selection at eleven. This differentiation by arbitrary measurement of
ability contrasts sharply with comprehensivation in England and
Wales. However not only is education in the province elitist in the sense
that some pupils are annually creamed off, but the process of selection
and segregation highlights the realities of working in the classroom in
Northern Ireland. On the one hand primary education is dominated
by 'testing' if not in curricular terms, rather in the practicalities of the
availability of relatively 'easy' measures of successful teaching which are
commonly used as popular evaluations of schools. While, on the other
hand, secondary education is crudely differentiated by grammar and
secondary schools and by social class differences among pupils.

The easy predictiveness of high academic attainment through grammar schooling is an illustration of how difficult it has been to break out
of the 'stranglehold' of testing at eleven. Critics of selection fall into two
groups. Firstly, those who argue for a more equitable system, that is, an
efficient and effective process of differentiation by ability. Criticism of
selection from this quarter has led to the constant rethinking and fine-
tuning of the administration of the process. Secondly, those who
argue that selection is ideologically unsound and who point to the
predictability of social class and home/background influences on test
scores. This issue is the one which faces education squarely as the
National Curriculum and assessment become a reality. Will assessment
at 8, 11, 14 and 16 years improve the delivery of education? Schools in
Northern Ireland have been testing for over 40 years and children still
fail to achieve satisfactory standards. Would, for example, systematic
testing improve education in west Belfast?

While the nature of a selective system creates and labels different
school types, differences exist within schools. For example, in the primary sector a continuing debate addresses the question of 'coaching'
for the tests. The amount of preparation for the test, the type of prepa-

ration and the place of 'coaching' on the curriculum varies across the province. But coaching does exist and is a significant influence in schools. The demand from parents for grammar school places reinforces and accentuates the apparent need in schools for 'thorough' preparation for the selection tests. Schools which 'coach' extensively are popularly labelled 'good schools'.

In the secondary sector the differences between school types are most marked. Pupils attending grammar schools have access to a wider and more balanced curriculum even allowing for a lack of commercial and technological subjects. They are also all expected to sit for GCSE examinations or equivalent and to do so in more subjects than children in the non-grammar school sector. Since academic success is the yardstick by which schools are judged it is apparent that in the parents' eyes parity of esteem simply does not exist.

The route described in 'The Way Forward' will lessen but not eradicate the differences between the grammar and the secondary intermediate school sectors. The introduction of a free-market philosophy for school enrolments where physical capacity will be the only limiting factor will have far-reaching effects on schools. Popular schools will grow at the expense of other schools. Curriculum provision will be even more sharply differentiated as some schools grow and the others find it increasingly difficult to offer even the core subjects as pupil – and staff – numbers decline. In Northern Ireland, a tradition exists of large, academically-oriented grammar schools. These schools have the capacity to expand in a competitive market at the expense of the non-grammar school sector. However, since this means opening their doors to a less highly selected group of pupils one is left to ponder, will the stranglehold of selection be broken at last?

Selection in the school system, however, has provided a means whereby some pupils have crossed cultural divisions. Curricular limitations in some Catholic schools have led to some Catholic pupils going to state-controlled schools. Even if the movement is one dimensional, it does break the cultural monopoly of school management and, indeed, in some cases 'ownership'. Schools provide the means of identifying cultural differences in this province. This has been institutionalised by the Fair Employment Agency's use of primary school attended as the test of ethnicity to monitor selection and promotion in employment in the province.

Schools are an important means whereby cultural identity is reinforced. Catholics and Protestants live and learn in socio-cultural locations that through the curriculum and para-curriculum local schools socialise participants into an unquestioning acceptance of the existing level of cultural separation. However, selection at eleven, perceived social status and altruism has created a small but expanding integrated school movement. This movement is, as yet, mainly one-sided – Catholic to integrated – and does not reflect a universal demand to break with the traditional forms of school management. However, it does present the 'seeds' of a movement for change albeit in what is historically infertile ground.

Northern Ireland has a multitude of small schools (43% of all primary schools have enrolments of 100 pupils or less). The case for closing small schools rests on a number of assertions. DENI (1981) argued in a policy document on school closures that demographic trends and pupil numbers were the sole basis of decision-making. What the document did not clarify was the Inspetorate's belief that in a school of four or less teachers, a weak teacher had a considerable impact on academic attainment. The policy was, therefore, to increase the size of the school and subsequently reduce the potential influence of any individual teacher. The Department in 1984 named 187 primary schools it regarded as 'ripe' for closure (Eliott *et al.*, 1988). This represented 17% of the primary school stock.

Central to the debate about ongoing school rationalisation lies the question of attainment and educational opportunity. This has been highlighted in recent concern about attainment levels at school leaving of pupils in the province. For whatever reason, the more able child does better at school in Northern Ireland than his counterparts elsewhere while the less able does less well in terms of certification. As in other industrial conurbations in Britain, there is a concentration of adolescents in Belfast who are becoming increasingly disaffected by schooling. The response of schools has been to review practice concentrating on curricular provision. This approach has led to schools incorporating a number of initiatives designed to broaden their appeal in terms of what is offered through the curriculum to young people. If this approach is to succeed these schools must be able to circumvent all the other pressures facing adolescents today. Clearly curriculum alone is not a magic wand that puts everything right in the garden. A broader, more structured and balanced approach is needed incorporating the psychological needs of young people, an appreciation of the demands regularly made of pupils at school and home and a sensitivity to the developing adult. Any one of these factors has enormous implications for the management of the curriculum in schools.

Schools, in general, and the curriculum, in particular, have been slow to change in Northern Ireland. The service is locked into an academic and subject-oriented vice. It is not surprising that the attempt at curriculum development in primary schools was set into individual and, indeed, self-contained disciplinary compartments in the Primary Guidelines. Much of the impact of the Schools Council work was lost on a system prepared to accept being judged on the basis of a few carefully selected, academically gifted and well-motivated children.

Throughout the eighties the question facing school authorities in the province was how to retain the academic achievement of a selected few and simultaneously manage the consequences of the system that chose to select by ability. Thus the process of change was targeted at those issues which teachers saw as difficult to handle. In the primary school a new degree of clarity was sought through the Primary Guidelines which, it was argued, would ease some of the pressures in preparing children for the selection tests. Less able children in the secondary school in their lack of acceptable outcomes created their own degree of pressure and a sensitive response was needed. Again this was through the curriculum and continued attempts to make it more 'appropriate'.

It is ironic that education in the nineties following the Reform Order will reverse much that the system/service set out to achieve in the eighties. Outcomes will no longer be problematic; processes, however, will be put firmly into the hands of teachers. Structures, sacrosanct in the eighties, will emerge in the nineties as a new realism pervades a service that has for too long depended on a few pupils for its academic reputation. Curriculum targets will apply to all children, not just those perceived to be of examination calibre.

Schools in the eighties were grappling with the prevalence of underachieving and a large number of disaffected pupils. This situation was accentuated by youth unemployment and a continuing limitation of opportunity which was rigidly held in place by sectarian violence. The Youth Training Programme attempted to compensate for some of the inadequacies of schooling by adopting an end-on approach which incorporated a period of work experience supported by some further education.

YTP found itself picking up a majority of young people who had found schooling inappropriate to their needs. This meant that the scheme had to spend much of its time trying to redress the balance of young people's perception of education. Commentators continually identify selection at eleven as the cause of so much client dissatisfaction with schools. However, it remains to be seen as educational change occurs if schools through their organisational structures have created forms of pupil disaffiliation, or if young wage labour will continue to dismiss schools as irrelevant in their lives.

There is not a great deal of evidence to show that change has occurred at a level of classroom practice in the eighties. While Primary Guidelines and the 11–16 Programme can sustain a claim to have created a number of structures in schools, curriculum co-ordinators, curriculum committees, pastoral systems and committees formed to discuss record-keeping and achievement profiles, these can appear not to-have directly influenced classroom practice. Whole school review while a valuable theoretical exercise, has not of itself affected a 'change of heart' in the classroom. Clearly this strategy needed a more flexible and varied approach if it was to influence teachers. The preoccupation to relate in-service education, school-based approaches with system-based need has a certain theoretical soundness yet it has failed to address how developmental strategy can be transformed into a set of tactical exercises and implemented in classrooms.

All too frequently the logistics of the job of teaching, the pressures of the classroom, the children's values or even crass optimism among administrators have locked practising teachers into a 'here and now' world from which there was little escape. The gap between the top-down approaches adopted by the regional curriculum development schemes and the classroom appear to have reinforced a set of structures around classroom practitioners that denied teachers scope for experimentation and evaluation. Thus education has found it difficult to break out of the stranglehold of existing modes of practice. While systematic regional initiatives found it difficult to reach into the classroom, teachers found it equally difficult to identify a means of expression that would liberate them from the constraints of accepted organisational practice and the obvious structural limitations imposed both by selection and segregation. However, if divisions among schools by selection have not been healed by attempts to modify the curriculum, the divisions by religion are a long way from being cured by integration of different religious denominations.

What then of the future and the educational reforms proposed as 'The Way Forward'? At one level this initiative addresses under-achievement directly and picks up the issue which the regional curriculum development initiatives continually refused to consider. Testing and assessment as proposed by the Order are not new or innovative in Northern Ireland. Here the system of schools is fine-tuned to the nuances of test scores and inter-school comparisons. Some schools have developed academic reputations on the relative achievements of their more capable pupils. Others have suffered because of having reputations for indiscipline and condoning unsocial behaviour. Only the future can tell if systematic assessment at regular intervals will lead to the emergence of a system that is different from the present one.

As the implementation of the Education Reform Order approaches two issues remain unanswered. In the context of working in a school in Northern Ireland how will selection and segregation by ability be affected by systematic assessment? Will testing become the diagnostic influence that will not only measure attainment but also make a positive contribution to learning? Can parents be encouraged to see regular assessment as more than a measure of success or failure? How can those that manage schools ensure that testing is a positive force and not just another means of separating 'Tim from Tom'? If the case studies reported earlier in 'Schools under Scrutiny' are indicative of practice there is little evidence to support an ideology which purports to centralise curriculum while simultaneously decentralising control.

Secondly, what is the future of the integrated school? In this instance it is left to parents to influence those who manage schools in the province to provide a form of education that does not subscribe to the traditions of ownership and control. The Reform Order allows for local control, but what if neighbourhood management is sectarian in character? Will parent governers lock schools into the socio-cultural space of the neighbourhood?

At all levels in the education service administrators, teachers and parents are having to re-evaluate their positions on schooling. Implicit in the present reforms is the goal of a business-orientated, scientifically-based and attainment-driven school. Are children to be consumed by the world of work, a technological environment and attainment targets? Can we not ask ourselves if there is more to schools than this? Aren't children people too? Can they not make a contribution to how they see their worlds and indeed their schools?

Bibliography

Advisory Council for Education in Northern Ireland 1952. *Selection of Pupils: Secondary Schools*. Belfast: HMSO Cmd. 301.

Advisory Council for Education in Northern Ireland 1955. *Selection of Pupils: Secondary Schools*. Second Report. Belfast: HMSO Cmd. 335.

Advisory Council for Education in Northern Ireland 1960. *Selection of Pupils for Secondary Schools*. Third Report. Belfast: HMSO Cmd 419.

Advisory Council for Education in Northern Ireland 1964. *Four Short Reports: Secondary School Organisation*, Conditions of Recognition, Supply of Teachers and Selection Procedure. Belfast: HMSO Cmd. 471.

Advisory Council for Education in Northern Ireland 1971. *The Existing Selection Procedure for Secondary Education in Northern Ireland*. Belfast: HMSO Cmd. 551.

Advisory Council for Education in Northern Ireland 1973. Reorganisation of Secondary Education in Northern Ireland 'The Burges Report'. Belfast: HMSO Cmd. 574.

AGBVS, 1977. *The Future of Education in Northern Ireland*. Belfast.

Akenson, D.H. 1973. Education and Enmity. Newtown Abbot: David and Charles. New York: Barnes and Noble.

Armstrong, R. 1979. *Through the Ages to Newtownabbey*. Belfast: Shanway Publications.

Ashton, P. 1975. *Aims in practice in the Primary School*. London: University Press.

Aston University, 1981. *The Social Effects of Rural Primary School Reorganisation*. Final Report. Birmingham: University of Aston.

Barker Lunn 1984. Junior School Teachers: Their Methods and Practices. *Educational Research*. 26, pp. 178–188.

Bell, A. and Sigworth, A. 1987. *The Small Rural Primary School: A Matter of Quality*. London: Falmer Press.

Benn, J. 1969. Comprehensive Education – The Northern Ireland Situation in Rhodes, E. (ed.) *Comprehensive Secondary Education*. Londonderry: Magee University College.

Bennett, S.N. 1987. Task Process in Mixed and Single Age Classes. *Education, 3–13*, March.

Bernstein, B.B. 1971. On the Classification and Framing of Educational Knowledge in Young, MFD 1971, *Knowledge and Control*. London: Macmillan.

Blyth, W.A.L. 1965. *English Primary Education: A Sociological Analysis*. Volume 11: Background. London: Routledge and Kegan Paul.

Board of Education, 1905. *Handbook of Suggestions*. London: HMSO.

Bobbit, J.F. 1918. *How to Make a Curriculum*. New York: Houghton Mifflin.

Bolton, E.P. 1985. Curriculum 5–16, *Educational Review* 37(3), pp.199–215.

Bowles, S. and Gintis, H. 1976. *Schooling in Capitalist America*. London: Routledge and Kegan Paul.

Boyd, G.H.S., 1972. Socio-Economic and Educational Factors Influencing the Decline of the One-two-and-three Teacher Elementary School in Northern Ireland since Partition, with Reference to Current Trends in Great Britain and the Republic of Ireland. Unpublished PhD Thesis, Queen's University, Belfast.

Burke, A. and Fontes, P.J. 1986. Educational Beliefs and Practices of Sixth Class Teachers in Irish Primary Schools. *The Irish Journal of Education*, 20(1&2), pp. 51–77.

Campbell, R.J. 1985. *Developing the Primary Curriculum*. London: Holt, Rinchart and Winston.

Cathcart, H.R. 1984. *The Most Contrary Region: The BBC in Northern Ireland 1924–1984*. Belfast, Blackstaff Press.

Caul, L. and Harbison, J. 1986, *Condoned Absenteeism*. Belfast: Stranmillis College.

Charters, W.W. 1923. *Curriculum Construction*. New York: Macmillan Ltd.

Chilver Report 1982. *The Future of Higher Education in Northern Ireland*. Belfast: HMSO.

Darby J. and Dunn, S. 1987. Segregated Schools: The Research Evidence in Osborne, R., Cormack, R. and Miller R. 1987. *Education and Policy in Northern Ireland*. Belfast: Policy Research Institute.

Darby, J. 1986. *Intimidation and the Control of Conflict in Northern Ireland*. Dublin: Gill and Macmillan.

Daws, P.P. 1987. *Citizenship in the Post Primary School Curriculum*. Address to British Association for the Advancement of Science, Education Section. Belfast: August, 1987.

Department of Economic Development/Department of Education for Northern Ireland DED/DENI 1988. *Youth Training Programme: Review 1987–1988:* Plan 1988–1989.

Department of Education NI 1974. *Programme for Primary Schools*. Belfast: HMSO.

Department of Education NI 1978. *Persistent School Absenteeism in Northern Ireland*. Belfast: Department of Finance NI.

Department of Education NI 1981. *Primary Education*: Report of an Inspectorate Survey in Northern Ireland. Belfast: HMSO.

Department of Education NI 1983. *Persistent School Absenteeism in Northern Ireland*. Belfast: Department of Finance and Personnel NI.

Department of Education NI 1983. *Demographic Trends*. Belfast: HMSO.

Department of Education NI 1984. *Secondary Schools: A New Development for the 11-16 Year Olds*. Belfast.

Department of Education NI 1985. *The Youth Training Programme in Five Colleges*. DENI: Rathgael House, Bangor.

Department of Education NI 1988. Education Reform in Northern Ireland: *The Way Forward*. Belfast: HMSO.

Department of Education and Science 1978. *Curriculum 11-16:* Working Papers by HMI – A Contribution to Current Debate. London: HMSO. 1978.

Department of Education and Science 1978. *Primary Education in England*. London: HMSO.

Department of Education and Science 1980. Mathematical Development: *Secondary Science Report* No 1. A.P.U. London: HMSO. 1980.

Department of Education and Science 1985. *Better Schools*. London: HMSO. Cmd. 9469.

Driver, R., Head, J. and Johnson, S. 1984. The Differential Uptake of Science in England, Wales and Northern Ireland. *European Journal of Science Education*, 6(1), 19–29.

Dunn, S. 1986. The Education Debate in Northern Ireland: The Integrated Option. *Education Studies*, 75, 299.

Elliot, S., O'Leary, C. and Wilford, R.A. 1988. *The Northern Ireland Assembly 1982-1986*. London: C. Hurst and Company.

Friere, P., 1972. *Pedagogy of the Oppressed*. Penguin Books.

Gallagher, A.M. 1988. *Transfer Pupils at Sixteen*. Report No. 4 from the NICER Transfer Procedure Project. Belfast: Northern Ireland Council for Educational Research.

Gallagher, A.M. 1989. The Impact of Research on Policy: An Example from Northern Ireland, *The Psychologist*, 2(2), 62–63.

Galton, M. 1987. Unpublished Report on Small Primary Schools. London: DES.

Gittins Report, CACE, Wales 1967. *Primary Education in Wales*. London: HMSO.

Hadow Report, 1931. *Report of the Consultative Committee on the Primary School.* London: HMSO.

Halsey, A.H., Heath, A. and Ridge, J.M., 1980. *Origins and Destinations.* London: Clarendon Press.

HMI, 1978. *Primary Education in England.* London: HMSO.

HMI, 1984. *Educational Provision and Response in Some Norfolk Schools.* Report by H.M. Inspectors. London: HMSO.

Hopson, B., and Scally, M. 1981. *Lifeskills Teaching.* McGraw-Hill Books.

Jencks, C., *et al.* 1973. *Inequality: A Reassessment of Effects of Family and Schooling in America.* London: Allen Lane.

King, R. 1978. *All Things Bright and Beautiful? A Sociological Study of Infants' Classrooms.* London: John Wiley and Sons.

Livingstone, J. 1987. Equality of Opportunity in Education in Northern Ireland in Osborne, R.D., Cormack, R.J. and Miller, R.L. *Education and Policy in Northern Ireland.* Policy Research Institute, The Queen's University of Belfast and the University of Ulster.

Loughran, G. 1987. The Rationale of Catholic Education in Osborne, R., Cormack, R. and Miller, R. *Education and Policy in Northern Ireland.* Belfast: Policy Research Institute, Queen's University and University of Ulster.

Malone, J.M. 1988. *Schools Project in Community Relations.* Belfast: John Malone Memorial Trust.

Maslow, A.H. 1968. *Towards a Psychology of Being.* 2nd ed. New York: Van Nostrand Reinhold.

Maslow, A.H. 1970. *Motivation and Personality.* 2nd ed. New York: Harper and Row.

Miliband, R. 1969. *The State in Capitalist Society.* London: Quartet Books.

Ministry of Education, Northern Ireland 1932. *Programme of Instruction for Public Elementary Schools.* Belfast: HMSO.

Ministry of Education, Northern Ireland 1956. *Programme for Primary Schools.* Belfast: HMSO.

Ministry of Education, Northern Ireland 1966. *Education in Northern Ireland in 1965.* Report of the Ministry of Education. Belfast: HMSO. Cmd. 492.

Ministry of Education, Northern Ireland 1967. *Selection Procedure for Secondary Education.* Bangor: Ministry of Education Circular No. 1967/55.

McWhirter, L. 1989. *Longitudinal Evidence on Teenage Years.* Belfast: Northern Ireland Office, Planning and Policy Unit.

McElligott, T.J. 1981. *Secondary Education in Ireland.* 1870–1921. Dublin: Irish Academic Press.

McEwen, A. 1985. Teacher Values: A Case Study of Northern Ireland Teachers. *Educational Research*. NFER Vol. 27, No. 1, pp. 19–22.

McEwen, A. and Curry, C.A. 1986. Subject Preferences at 'A' Level in Northern Ireland, *European Journal of Science Education*, Vol. 8, No. 1, pp. 39–50.

NIACRO, 1981. *Unemployment and Young Offenders in Northern Ireland*. Belfast: NIACRO.

Northern Ireland Council for Educational Development 1985. *Guidelines for Primary Schools*: Introduction, Health and Social Education, History, Mathematics, Language and Literacy, Music, Physical Education, Science and Geography. Belfast: NICED.

Northern Ireland Council for Educational Development 1985. *Primary Guidelines*. Belfast: NICED.

Northern Ireland Council for Educational Development 1986. External Evaluation Report. Belfast: NICED.

Northern Ireland Council for Educational Development 1989. *The Role of the Principal in Review and Development*. Primary Guidelines Support Paper. Belfast: NICED.

O'Buachalla, S. 1988. *Education Policy in Twentieth Century Ireland*. Dublin: Wolfhound.

Osborne, R., Cormack R. and Miller, R. 1987. *Education and Policy in Northern Ireland*. Belfast: Policy Research Institute, Queen's University and University of Ulster.

Parliament of Northern Ireland 1959, 1963. *Parliamentary Debates Hansard*, 44, 768–776 and 53, 865–913.

Plowden Report, CACE 1967. *Children and Their Primary School*. London: HMSO.

Regional Curriculum Base 1988. *Youthways: A Staff Development Review*. University of Ulster, Jordanstown.

Reid, J. 1987. Religiously Integrated Schools: A Parental Perspective, unpublished M.Ed. Thesis, School of Education, Queen's University of Belfast.

Reid, K. 1985. *Truancy and School Absenteeism*. London: Hodder and Stoughton.

Robinson, A. 1971. *Education and Sectarian Conflict in Northern Ireland* New Era 52.1.

Robinson, A. 1988. The Condition of Education for Mutual Understanding in Robinson, A. (ed.) *Education for Mutual Understanding – Roles and Responsibilities*. Coleraine: University of Ulster.

Ross, C. 1988. Clarity Begins at Home. *Youth in Society*. October 1988, p. 24.

Rutter, M. *et al.* 1979. *Fifteen Thousand Hours.* London: Open Books.

Salters, J. 1970. Attitudes Towards Society Among Protestant and Catholic Schoolchildren in Belfast, unpublished M.Ed. Thesis, School of Education, Queen's University of Belfast.

Scott, N. 1985. Speech by the Under-Secretary of State for Education at Omagh Academy Prize-giving. Times Educational Supplement, 15 November 1987.

Schools Council 1981. Working Paper 70. *The Practical Curriculum.* London: Methuen Education.

Schools Council 1983. Working Paper 75. *Primary Practice.* London: Methuen Education.

Scottish Education Department 1980. Learning and Teaching in Primary 4 and Primary 7: A Report by HM Inspectors of Schools in Scotland. Edinburgh: HMSO.

Scottish Education Department 1974. *Education in Inverness-shire.* Edinburgh: HMSO.

Sher, J.D. 1981. *Rural Education in Urbanised Nations.* OCED/CERI Report.

Spencer, AECW 1987. Arguments for an Integrated School System in Osborne, R., Cormack, R. and Miller, R. *Education and Policy in Northern Ireland.* Belfast: Policy Research Institute Queen's, University and University of Ulster.

Steadman, S.D. *et al.* 1981. *The Schools Council, Its Take-up in Schools and General Impact.* A Final Report. London: Schools Council.

Steward, D.J. and Prebble, T.K. 1984. *Making It Happen: A School Development Process.* Palmerston North: Dunmore Press Ltd, Canberra.

Sullivan, M. 1987. Working and Learning in Other People's Classrooms. *Education 3–13.* October 1987, pp. 10–12.

Sutherland, A.E. 1981. *Curriculum Projects in Primary Schools.* Belfast: NICER.

Sutherland, A.E. and Gallagher, A.M. 1986. *Transfer and the Upper Primary School.* Report No. 1 from the NICER Transfer Procedure Project. Belfast: Northern Ireland Council for Educational Research.

Sutherland, A.E. and Gallagher, A.M. 1987. *Pupils in the Boarder Band.* Report No. 3 from the NICER Procedure Project. Belfast: Northern Ireland Council for Educational Research.

Teare, S.M. and Sutherland, A.E. 1988. *At Sixes and Sevens: A Study of the Curriculum in the Upper Primary School.* Report No. 5 from the NICER Transfer Procedure Project. Belfast: Northern Ireland Council for Educational Research.

Titley, E.B. 1983. *Church, State and the Control of Schooling in Ireland 1900–*

1944. Kingston and Montreal: Gill and Macmillan.

Tyler, R.W. 1948. *Basic Principles of Curriculum and Instruction*. University of Chicago Press.

Tyerman, M.J. 1968. *Truancy*. London: University of London Press.

Wallace, I.H.N. 1984. Education in the 1990s and Beyond in The Future of Education in Northern Ireland. Conference: DENI and Ulster Bank.

Welsh Office 1986. A Survey of Primary Schools in Part of the Borough of Torfaen, Gwent: A Report by HM Inspectors. Cardiff: Welsh Office.

Whately, R. 1832. Letter to the Dean of St Patrick's Cathedral, Dublin, 18 January 1832. In the Possession of H.R. Cathcart.

Wilson, J.A. and Spelman, B.J. 1977. *The Organisation of Secondary Education*. Belfast: Northern Ireland Council for Educational Research.

Wilson, J.A. 1985. *Secondary School Organisation and Pupil Progress*. Belfast: Northern Ireland Council for Educational Research.

Wilson, J.A. 1986. *Transfer and the Structure of Secondary Education*: Report No. 2 from the NICER Transfer Procedure Project. Belfast: Northern Ireland Council for Educational Research.

Wilson, J.A. 1989. Educational Performance: A Decade of Evidence in Harbison, J. (ed.) *Growing Up in Northern Ireland*. Belfast: Learning Resources Unit, Stranmillis College.

Index